FAITH BOOKS & SPIRITUAL JOURNALING

other and Forgive whatever grievances you have against one another. Forgive as the Lord forgave you. And... put on love, which binds them all together in perfect unity. Col. 3:13-14

"Sing to the Lord with thanksgiving..." Ps 147:7

Joyful Heart

:17 Every good gift and every perfect gift is from above, and cometh down from the Father of lights, with whom is no variableness, neither shadow of turning.

FAITH BOOKS & SPIRITUAL JOURNALING

Expressions of Faith through Art

GLOUCESTER MASSACHUSETTS

QUARRY BOOKS

SHARON SONEFF

Inspirational Entries by Mindy Caliguire

First published in the United States of America by

Quarry Books, a member of

Quayside Publishing Group

33 Commercial Street

Gloucester, Massachusetts 01930-5089

Telephone: (978) 282-9590

Fax: (978) 283-2742

www.rockpub.com

Library of Congress Cataloging-in-Publication Data

Soneff, Sharon.

    Faith books and spiritual journaling : expressions of faith through art
/ Sharon Soneff.

        p.   cm.

    ISBN 1-59253-268-3 (pbk.)

    1. Spiritual life—Christianity. 2. Spiritual journals—Authorship. 3.
Handicraft—Religious aspects—Christianity. I. Title.

    BV4501.3.S658 2006

    248.4'6—dc22   2006010356

                                                            CIP

ISBN-13: 978-1-59253-268-1

ISBN-10: 1-59253-268-3

10 9 8 7 6 5 4 3 2 1

Design: Laura H. Couallier, Laura Herrmann Design
Photography: Allan Penn

Printed in Singapore

"But you desire honesty from the heart, so you can teach me to be wise in my inmost being."

PSALM 51:6

CONTENTS

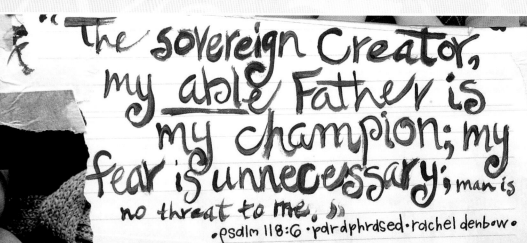

"The sovereign Creator, my able Father is my champion; my fear is unnecessary; man is no threat to me."

– psalm 118:6 • paradphrased • rachel denbow •

ALeXa
AiDaN

There are times when God's still small VOICE SPEAKS loud & clear. These precious children belong to Him. By example, I need to constantly FUEL their FAITH to HOPE TRUST and BeLiEVe.

Call to me & I will answer ~ tell

Deuteronomy 11:18*20

Fix these words of mine in your hearts and minds as symbols on

C 1413 II

FOREWORD

By Mindy Caliguire

*Y*ou hold in your hands a resource that could literally change your life. Few books claim to offer such hope, and fewer still actually deliver. What makes this book different? Beyond the beautiful photos and inspirational ideas, what lurks within these pages is actually an invitation. *Faith Books & Spiritual Journaling* will mean nothing to you if, through it, you do not hear and respond to a strong and insistent whisper: *What's your story? What's your experience of God? What is real for you?*

Accepting this invitation will allow you to attend to a deeper experience of your spiritual journey. If you let it, the art of *Faith Books & Spiritual Journaling* can drive you further into the art that is your own life—the unique person God is forming and making as *you*. Any time you accept an invitation to a deeper relationship with this amazing God who loves you—watch out! Things deep within your soul can begin to shift. Change. Become free. Grow....

The following pages explode with ideas, color, shapes, texture, dimensions, and creativity! You will see what our artists have expressed out of the depth of their relationships with God and now offer to you. But remember that this is *your invitation.*

So what will your faith book record? On which days will you choose to write a gratitude list and surround it with antique lace or balloons? On which days will you choose a red or gold Crayola crayon and color outside the lines? On which days will you allow your heart to bleed on paper with fears or pain? On which days will you creatively present a scripture verse that God ambushed you with?

I cannot answer those questions for you. But I can promise that as you discern and then creatively express the truth of your faith journey on paper, your heart will become increasingly open and your spiritual growth will become more solid. Generations have come to understand the truth: "Seek and you will find." Your faith book will honor and highlight what you have discovered along your path.

I urge you to take the time and create the space to become a student of the works presented here. Explore them. Ask yourself, "What do I see?" "How does this touch me?" Then, become a student of your own living work of art: your experience of life with God. Do this, and your faith book will become a sacred place to record and request, to highlight and honor, to celebrate and surrender to the movement of God in your life.

Are you ready to accept this invitation? I hope you will. You have every reason to expect to be surprised, challenged, and delighted by your experience creating a faith book. You'll have a beautiful, permanent record of God's own work of art lovingly expressed and recorded as part of your amazing journey of faith.

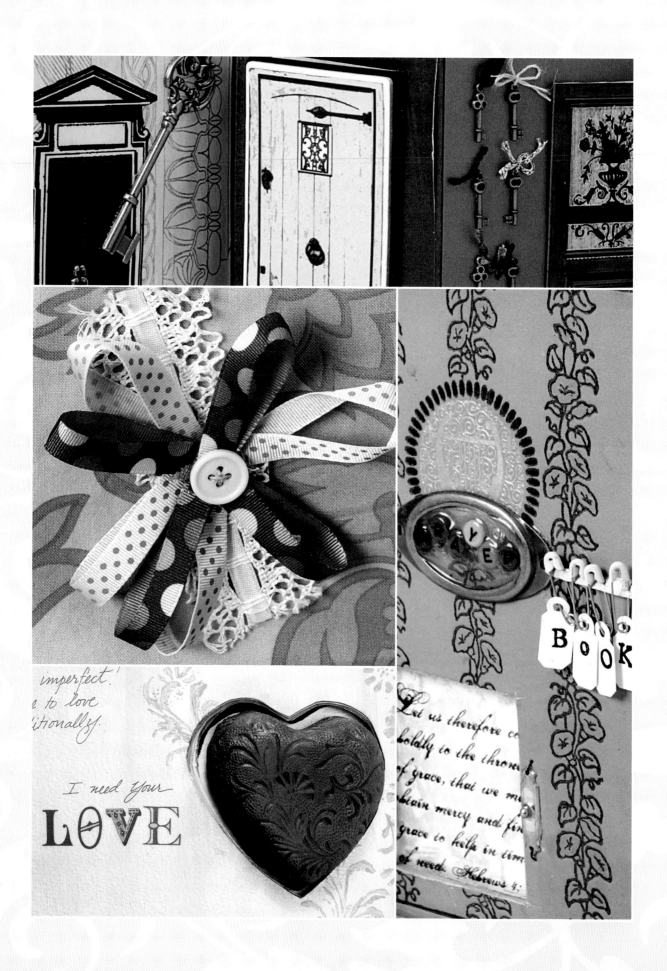

Chapter 1
PRAYER BOOKS

Introduction by Mindy Caliguire

If you've been around the religious world for any length of time, you most likely have had assorted experiences with prayer. You may recall services marked by seemingly endless and possibly formulaic prayer. Some people repeat rehearsed phrases that feel cliché, overly sentimental, or even shallow. You may have voiced such prayers yourself. Many of us have gone through the motions before a meal or even when alone before bedtime. But in many cases, we don't really feel free to express our truest thoughts and feelings. Is that allowed? Can we be completely "honest to God?"

The answer is yes. And that's why the following pages are so valuable.

If you read the prayers recorded on the pages of the Bible, you may be surprised to discover a very different kind of prayer. It's the prayer expressed in the Psalms with words such as: "Out of the depths I cry to you, Lord…" (Psalm 130:1). Elsewhere the author of these psalms prays, "I know that You (God) desire truth in the innermost parts!" Imagine that—this person fully believed that **God really wanted people to freely express themselves in all honesty and from the "innermost parts!"** He wanted a relationship of prayer.

That kind of prayer can't be fabricated or ornamental. It can't be forced or rehearsed. So finding your true "prayer voice" for speaking to God is worth the challenge. As you discover a way to access the *place* from which authentic prayer emerges, you will begin to speak to God from the place of the soul. The truest part of who you are.

Explore these heart-felt and soul-baring prayer projects and allow yourself to be challenged by the authenticity of the examples given. Then search the depths of *your* soul and offer up whatever you find there. What is the honest cry that lives deep within you? It might be a cry for help, or a cry for mercy, or a cry for forgiveness. You may find inside a cry for healing, or for protection, or even a loud and raucous cry of praise and thanksgiving!

Then, go for it! Visually express the cry that emerges out of the depths of your heart with terrific energy and even a little pizzazz. It's not that you'll impress God or anyone else with the beauty you create. Instead, you will honor and acknowledge the truth of your life and the courageous decision you made to offer your heart to God in prayer. Over time, your faith will expand as you see how God responds specifically to your requests.

Regardless of what specific words emerge from the depths of your heart, be assured that God hears, God cares, and God responds to each and every one. Your prayer book creates a tribute to this One who hears every cry—from the very depths of your heart—with perfect attentiveness and unwavering love.

BELOW The cover of this shimmering journal features both metallic and interference acrylic paints, tapestry ribbons, and a hand-formed clay heart to express a sacred tone.

The Cry of My Heart
JOURNAL

ARTIST: *Sharon Soneff*

SOMETIMES A PRAYER IS NOTHING MORE THAN AN OUT-crying of the heart. Those cries can be vocalized in spoken words, but they can also be expressed with pens, paints, and papers applied to the pages of a journal, as shown here. A symbolic embossed clay heart peeking through every page reminds us that the heart is the centerpiece for this personal account of prayers. Surrounding the clay heart are page after page of artistic expressions reflecting what the heart needs from God. A plea of "I need Your strength," "I need Your mercy," or "I need Your joy" finds a safe resting place between the protective covers of this spiral watercolor journal.

MATERIALS

spiral watercolor journal
air-dry clay
embossed papers
ribbon remnants
clear alphabet stickers
acrylic paints
   (metallic and non-metallic)
interference paint
gesso

TOOLS

mini heart cake form
   (Wilton)
hot knife cutting tool
   (Walnut Hollow Hot Marks)
micro-tip scissors
hot glue gun
glue stick
pencils
   (white and standard graphite)
brush
archival pen for journaling

"From the end of the earth will I cry unto thee, when my heart is overwhelmed: lead me to the rock that is higher than I."

PSALM 61:2

ABOVE An opening is cut through the front cover and every interior page to mirror the shape of the journal's central clay heart, allowing the form to show through from its place on the inside of the back cover.

1 Knead the air-dry clay and press it into a mini heart cake form. (HELPFUL TIP: Lining the cake form with a sheet of plastic wrap will help you remove the molded heart and minimize cleanup). Pull out the molded heart.

2 Lightly brush the clay heart with water to keep the surface malleable. While the clay is still soft and wet, place a piece of highly embossed decorative paper on top of the clay and press firmly. Continue to press the embossed motif of the paper onto the sides of the clay heart. Set the heart aside to dry. (Refer to manufacturer's label to determine drying time; this heart took nearly a week to harden for painting.)

3 For positioning purposes only, temporarily place the clay heart on top of the spiral journal cover and mark around it with a white pencil. Remove the heart and set aside.

4 With the pages turned back and out of the way, use a hot knife cutting tool, and retrace the marking of the heart shape on the cover with the heated blade. Use multiple slow, deliberate strokes of the knife to cut through the cover.

5 Using the void in the cover, trace the heart shape to the top page of watercolor paper in the journal. Cut out the traced heart in the page with micro-tipped scissors or a craft knife. Repeat this step for every page in the journal so there will be a heart-shaped void through the cover and every sheet until the back cover is reached. (The back cover will remain uncut.)

6 When the clay heart is thoroughly dry and hardened, apply gesso to seal it and then follow with two light coats of acrylic paint. An interference paint is used as a topcoat for a shimmering effect.

7 Using the heart-shaped cuts in the front cover and pages as a guide for placement, adhere the clay heart to the inside of the back cover with hot glue. Now, when the book is closed, the heart should protrude through every page and the front cover.

8 Apply gesso to the front cover and the internal pages to seal them before applying acrylic paints, papers, and stickers.

9 Referring to the photograph, apply a piece of decorative paper to part of the cover, and paint the remainder with a metallic acrylic paint. Where the paper and paint meet, adhere a ribbon with a hot glue gun for embellishment and to cover the seam.

10 Using clear alphabet stickers (rub-ons can also be used), spell out the title of the journal.

11 Continue to embellish the pages with personal journal entries illustrated further with patterned papers, paints, and ribbons.

BELOW Handwritten journaling is interspersed with titles punctuated by the use of clear alphabet stickers. Floral imagery is transferred to the journal by applying paint to embossed paper (the same embossed paper that was used to create the textural design on the clay heart) and then pressing it onto the journal's painted pages.

BELOW A wooden box accommodates a series of embellished prayer cards. Each card is filed behind monogrammed, tabbed dividers which designate the subject matter of the prayers.

Mini
PRAYER FILE

ARTIST: *Beth Wilkinson*

IN THIS CLEVER AND CRAFTY MINI FILE, THE ACRONYM J.O.Y. is used as a prompt to help us organize our prayers. "J" for "Jesus" reminds us to prioritize God first in all things, as even in prayer we are reminded to first pray words of thanks and worship to Him. "O" for "others" helps us to be diligent to intercede for the needs of friends and family members when we pray, rather than be simply self-focused. "Y" for "you" means that although we don't neglect ourselves by any means, we also submit our own needs to prayer. Using this acronym as a prayer prompt is not only a great aid but it also plainly spells out the result of keeping our life prioritized in such a fashion: *joy!*

The joy spelled out on the dividing cards of this prayer file also spills onto each of the prayer cards with colorful and playful expression. In jubilant and fashionable colors, the prayers are uniquely expressed on colored cards fashioned to fit on the internal dowels. Both useful and decorative, this prayer file takes the prayer journal beyond traditional book form.

MATERIALS

unfinished wooden box
dowels
metal plate
colored cardstock
ink-jet transparency sheets
patterned papers
scrapbook stickers
decorative brads
die-cut metal letters
Rolodex card
  (to use as a template)
scraps of lace and ribbon
personal photos
acrylic paint
clear, glossy varnish

TOOLS

wood glue
metal adhesive
paper adhesive
brush
Rolodex punching tool

"Confess your faults one to another, and pray one for another, that ye may be healed. The effectual fervent prayer of a righteous man availeth much."

JAMES 5:16

1 Paint the interior of the wooden box with an accent color of acrylic paint.

2 Adhere two pre-painted dowels stretching the length of the box using wood glue. Determine the spacing required between the dowels by using a card punched at the bottom with a Rolodex punching tool. When placed at the proper spacing, the punched notches of the card should rest tightly on the dowels.

3 Apply two to three coats of clear, glossy varnish to the entire piece.

4 Use metal adhesive to secure a decorative plate to the face of the box.

5 Using a Rolodex card as your template, cut three tabbed dividers from colored card-stock. On the first card, adhere a die-cut metal letter "j" to the far left of the tab using an adhesive suitable for metal to paper. On the second card, adhere a die-cut metal letter "o" to the top center of the tab. On the third card, adhere a die-cut metal letter "y" on the far right of the tab. When these three cards are viewed together, the metal letters will act as dividers, with the letters rising above the traditional tab. Notch the bottom of each card with the Rolodex punching tool.

BELOW Two dowels are positioned across a wooden box to provide a place for the notched prayer cards to rest. The base piece is given protection and beauty with applications of gloss lacquer.

6   To amplify and explain the letter dividers, type out the words "Jesus," "others," and "you" in decorative fonts and print them out on ink-jet transparency sheets. Trim and attach to the corresponding card using brads instead of adhesive (so the clarity of the transparency will not be clouded by glue or paste).

7   Create a series of prayer cards to insert in your file. Each can be uniquely embellished with photos, stickers, stamps, and ribbons. All will be notched with the punching tool for easy and secure attachment to the dowels.

ABOVE Cards adorned with patterned papers, brads, and stickers display expressions of prayer. The prayer cards of praises to God are filed behind the "Jesus" tab, while the prayer cards of needs for friends and family are filed behind the "others" tab. Expressions of prayers for oneself are filed behind the "you" tab.

Conversations with God
JOURNAL

ARTIST: *Elsie Flannigan*

WITH THE SHABBY CHARM AND EASE OF A SLIPCOVERED sofa, this slipcovered prayer journal feels like a comfortable friend at the very first glance. Inside, pages reveal entries that are just as relaxed, with their casually handwritten dialogues to God. This conversational style prayer journal speaks to the intimacy that God desires to have with us. Honest, raw, and transparent, the prayers are vulnerable reflections of the artist's desire to know God. But paired with bold and vibrant paints, applied with free abandon, the liberty to be entirely oneself with God is also clearly demonstrated. Not short on sass or spunk, this Conversations with God Journal is evidence that a prayer journal need not be stiff, formal, or sedate.

MATERIALS

spiral sketchbook
fabric remnant
ribbons
tulle
button
embroidery thread
acrylic paints
cardstock scraps
mini silk flowers
epoxy stickers
woven label tabs

TOOLS

scissors
adhesive
embroidery needle
stamps
archival pens for journaling
  (*black and opaque white*)
pins

"Draw near to God and He will draw near to you..."

JAMES 4:8

LORD, I FEEL SO CONFUSED. I WANT TO BE CLOSE TO YOU. I WANT TO BE A GOOD WIFE...AND I NEED YOU TO HELP ME FIND → SOME BALANCE...ONLY HUMAN IS SO CONFUSING COMPLICATED...→ I WANT TO DO THIS TOGETHER. I WANT TO LIVE IN FREEDOM AND HOPE AND JOY. I LOVE YOU! xxxxxx elsie

...i am and Life and → i want

i need you!

the truth is, i have always WANTED to be close to you, God. But sometimes I don't know how... i guess it's a journey. And that's O.k. ...

RIGHT Self-portraits and personal photos coupled with candid handwritten journaling aid in creating an extraordinarily intimate prayer book. This is your private, safe place, alone with God; don't be afraid to scribble and jot.

1. Lay the fabric remnant pattern-side down on a table. Fold the top of the fabric down and fold the bottom of the fabric up so that the overall height of the fabric matches the overall height of the spiral journal. Place the journal open on the fabric. Fold the excess fabric on the sides of the journal inward to create a pocket for insertion of the front and back covers. (Be sure there is enough room to fold the book closed.) Pin into place and set the journal aside.

2. Using a needle threaded with colorful embroidery thread, use large hand stitches to secure the side pockets of the fabric slipcover.

3. Loop ribbons to create a flower blossom. Secure onto the cover with a button and embroidery thread.

4. Insert the spiral journal into the fabric slipcover. Guide a ribbon remnant through the center of the spiral and tie it together on the outside edge of the journal. Hand write the word "prayers" onto a piece of cardstock. Secure the cardstock title by stitching through the cardstock, the ribbon, a snippet of tulle, and a small piece of the actual fabric cover.

5. Adorn internal pages with self-portraits and free-form applications of paint. Atop this surface, hand write or stamp your prayers and thoughts. Adhere photos and add handwritten thoughts and outlines directly to the photo's surface.

ABOVE Staggered pages, heart-shaped openings, doodled photos, and playfully scripted entries make this a happy home for free expression. Whimsy only adds to the attitude of abandon one should exercise when journaling with candor.

GALLERY

LEFT An assemblage of crosses crafted on the page encourages you to a place of confession. Recesses carved into thicknesses (where the book's pages have been adhered together) receive the protruding crosses fashioned from buttons and dried thorny rose branches.

ABOVE Filled to overflowing, this vintage book's pages lend residence to scenes of prayer. Complete with hinges and clasp, a door cut on the cover offers a peek into the contents within.

Altered
BOOK OF PRAYER

ARTIST: *Jennifer Hardy Williams*

A VINTAGE BOOK FINDS A SECOND LIFE AND purpose as an altered prayer book. Decked with charms and *ribbonerie,* the pages are loaded with embellishments, each detail together impelling a rich and meaningful prayer to God. An "A.C.T.S" prayer acronym was used to organize the artist's scenes ("A" for "adoration," "C" for "confession," "T" for "thanksgiving," and "S" for "supplication"). Secret compartments carved into a thickness of pages adhered together create perfect niches for private prayers professed to the heavenly Father.

ABOVE A masterfully collaged scene conjures imagery, and thus prayer, of adoration to God. The visual chanting of the word "holy" is typed in various fonts and printed onto a sheet of vellum. The holy scene is reinforced with a title of the same word spelled out in clear stickers and faux Scrabble tiles.

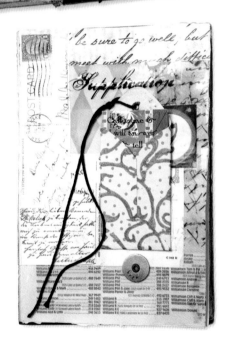

LEFT This sometimes-mysterious altered prayer book has many secret niches, compartments, and pockets for private prayers of supplication. On this page an envelope fashioned from patterned papers gives refuge to one such prayer.

BELOW Lush chocolate velvet ribbons hold a wire spiral where cards can be placed to declare thanksgiving to God. Even the simplest expression of gratitude has a grand position when placed here.

"Be anxious for nothing, but in everything by prayer and supplication, with thanksgiving, let your requests be made known to God; and the peace of God, which surpasses all understanding, will guard your hearts and minds through Christ Jesus."

PHILIPPIANS 4:6–7

RIGHT One end of the accordion journal features a small door where an image can be placed underneath. Shown here is an image copied from a vintage religious book, which perfectly resounds the accordion's "knocking" theme.

FAR RIGHT A miniature doorknob plate rests on the other end of the accordion journal, followed by panels with folded cardstock pieces atop them. Architectural door imagery is adhered to the top of each folded piece, while inside is a prayer that seeks God's will.

Knocking and Seeking
ACCORDION BOOK

ARTIST: *Sharon Soneff*

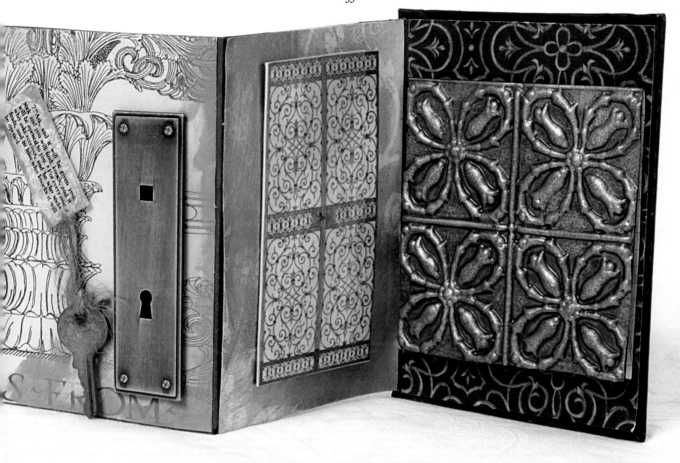

Like a metaphorical knock on God's door, this prayer journal adorned with a series of door images, door hardware, and key charms, was created to record those thumps at heaven's door made through "seeking" prayers. With a manufactured accordion book as a base structure, written prayer entries hide behind folded doors on each of the paper panels. Not only does the journal provide a place to express a prayer to God when He is needed to intervene and open doors, but the journal also serves to inspire your spirit, as the door imagery and key charms provide an aesthetic display of your creed.

"Ask, and it shall be given you; seek, and ye shall find; knock, and it shall be opened unto you."

MATTHEW 7:7

ABOVE A two-sided accordion book extends out to reveal numerous panels ornamented with door imagery, metal key charms, and miniature door hardware. The art and embellishments promote prayers that call on God to unlock doors in your life.

She Said/He Said
TAG BOOK

ARTIST: *Deb Perry*

ABOVE The commonalities of these two journals go beyond their flowered and beribboned qualities. Both of these prayer books are dedicated to recording God's communication to us.

ANOTHER KIND OF PRAYER JOURNAL IS ONE where the emphasis shifts from what we are asking for to what God is saying. Here, recording our needs and requests becomes secondary to recording that which God reveals to us. Whether it is through God's small voice speaking to your spirit or through His written word in scripture, God has something to say! The dialogue with God through prayer should not be a one-sided conversation. It is easy to find yourself in a place where you are rambling your requests to God, without taking pause to hear what His reply might be. Sitting still and silent before God's throne is another vital part of the practice of prayer.

BELOW Scrapbooking supplies like slide mounts, chipboard letters, and labeling tape compliment family photos and journaling where reflections of what God has to say about one's children are recorded.

These two journals make a special home for God's side of the conversation when we pray. In the "Be Still and Know that I Am God" journal, the entries are devoted to the practice of listening. The artist writes down things God says to her heart amidst illustrative photos and scrapbook embellishments. Similarly, in the "She Said/ He Said" tag book, earthly perspectives contrast sharply with heavenly perspectives. A "she said" entry (note the small "s" in she) on the left side of each tag records a commonly felt emotion (such as loneliness or weariness). But a powerful "He said" entry on the facing right tag records what God's scriptures tell us is His answer to these feelings. (Note that the use of the lowercase letter "s" in "she" acknowledges her humble admission of these human struggles.) This accessible format is a powerful tool for realizing God's concrete answers to our everyday struggles.

"Be still and know that I am God...."

PHILIPPIANS 46:10

she said...

"Lord, I am **W**ou**N**d**e**d yet I know that You do not desire me to take on this offense. Please help me to choose forgiveness rather than revenge or gossip. Help me to do this out of my Love for You, not because I have to."

ABOVE Tags on the left reveal the "she said" prayer, where vulnerable thoughts are written to God. Here, feelings of injury are exposed to God.

RIGHT Inked edges add a worn but loved look to this tag book. This homey trait introduces the sincere quality found in the pages within.

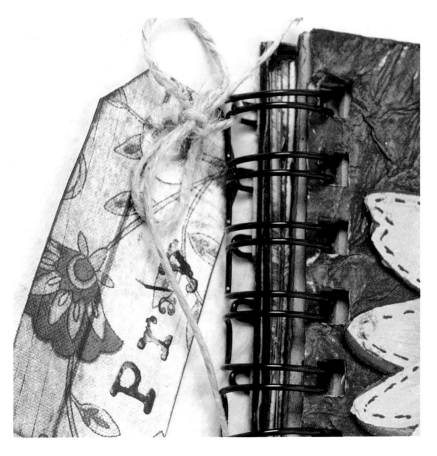

ABOVE Right-facing tags bear journaling that reveals the "He said" (or God's instruction as revealed in the Bible) response to the feelings expressed on the facing "she said" tag. A scripture that speaks to the wounded prayer lends instruction for forgiveness.

LEFT The use of commonly found materials, like the household twine that attaches a tag to the spine, gives the tag book familiarity and warmth.

Fear not, little flock, for it is the Father's good pleasure to give you the kingdom. Luke 12:32

Canvas
PRAYER BOARD

ARTIST: *Jennifer Hardy Williams*

A STRETCHED CANVAS BECOMES A PLACE TO literally pin your prayers. In this "beyond the book" prayer project, prayers are transcribed and artfully represented on a series of tags. Each tag represents a specific relationship or area of endeavor. (Tags seen here show prayers for a child, a spouse, a friend, work, research, and the leaders of our country, to name a few.) These tags are then attached with a pearl-topped corsage pin in rows of reminders across the canvas. As a visual illustration of God's perfect plans for our lives, the base canvas is covered with a sewing pattern tissue, providing a subtle but significant ground for the prayer tags.

ABOVE Each row of tags embodies prayers demonstrated through snippets of photos, stickers, scrapbook embellishments, and text. The open display of prayers serves as a reminder to *frequently* pray for a child, a spouse, leaders of government, and other people of importance.

RIGHT A corsage pin secures each tag to the canvas beneath. Here, a tag decorated with symbolic art and type reminds the artist to pray for the research ventures associated with her role as a college English professor.

"If any of you lacks wisdom, let him ask of God, who gives to all liberally and without reproach, and it will be given to him."

JAMES 1:5

Chapter 2
WORSHIP BOOKS

Introduction by Mindy Caliguire

Far from being a rare phenomenon, or limited to religious structures or events, the experience of worship is as natural as breathing. We're made for it. But, why, in fact, do we struggle to turn our attention to God in worship? Unfortunately, our soul's capacity to be enraptured is not terribly discriminating about the objects of our worship. If one could see the transcript of our daily thoughts and words, it would be clear that we devote much of our emotional and spiritual energy to people, things, and even ideas that become our mini-gods. The unintended objects of our worship.

Here's the catch: we eventually give ourselves over to whatever it is we worship. This puts us in a rather precarious place spiritually since we tend to worship things never intended to bear the full weight of a human soul. Still wondering what you might worship? Here are a few classic devotion-stealers: we worship careers, children, and causes; we worship body-types, fashion designers, and celebrities. We worship coffee, romantic relationships, ideas, and yes, even ourselves. The human soul is drawn to lose itself in the infinite "other." We are both profoundly capable and inwardly inclined to be consumed with love, admiration, desire, and devotion.

This tendency to give ourselves over to the object of worship is precisely why God, in tones of tender warning and concern, implores us to refrain from giving our worship to anything or anyone other than Himself. When we give ourselves over to a "lesser god" it is only a matter of time before the object of our worship is exposed in its insufficiency. And that moment can feel like death. And yes, very slowly perhaps at first, we can have the very life sucked out of us. Only the immensity, vastness, deep goodness, and fully aliveness of the living God can contain and fulfill the human soul.

So this chapter's invitation to you is this: create a beautiful worship faith book that inspires you to reflect on the goodness and majesty and power and compassion—the very person—of God. Create something that moves your heart to greater trust, greater love, greater courage, and greater faith. With great abandon, throw your whole heart into it. Into worship. Into God.

You'll be consumed by the very love that draws you to Itself, and you'll come away more like that love yourself. You will be transformed, in life-giving ways, by the object of your worship.

BELOW Covered with patterned papers bearing choral scores and illuminations, this old LP album is given a noble renovation. Gleaming gold details and rich hues give this project its simple sophistication.

Altered Vintage
LP ALBUM

ARTIST: *Sharon Soneff*

MATERIALS

vintage LP album
(found at online auction sites, flea markets, second-hand stores, and altered arts stores)

patterned papers

photographs, scans, or printed paper of stained glass imagery *(featured stained glass images are on transparency material)*

German Dresden gold foil paper borders

jacquard trim, metallic gimp, or braid

carbon transfer paper

acrylic paints
(gold metallic, red, blue, purple)

TOOLS

drafting tape

gold metallic paint pen
(fine tip)

pencil, ball-point pen, or ball-tipped burnishing tool

paintbrushes
(small, round-tipped brush for lettering, and medium to large flat brush for applying paste)

hot glue gun

archival paper paste

ARTISTS OF OLD OFTEN DEVOTED THEIR SKILL AND craft as an expression of worship to God. Grand ornate sculptures, masterpieces on canvas, and enormous cathedral ceilings were sometimes lifelong endeavors of artists whose only purpose was to glorify God. Using the finest materials and perfecting their craft was equivalent to an offering or tithe. This practice has seemingly been lost, but needlessly so. We all have been endowed with gifts to offer our King and our creative projects are a perfect place to express devotion to God. Here, a vintage LP album has been transformed into a piece of worshipful expression. The notebook-style album offers pages of an unusual format where worshipful words adorn the pages repetitively like a beautiful Gregorian chant. Text placed with varied scale and orientation becomes the primary art of this book, with support imagery peeking through the holes on each page where vinyl records once resided.

*"Give honor to the Lord for the glory of His name.
Worship the Lord in the splendor of His holiness."*

PSALM 29:2

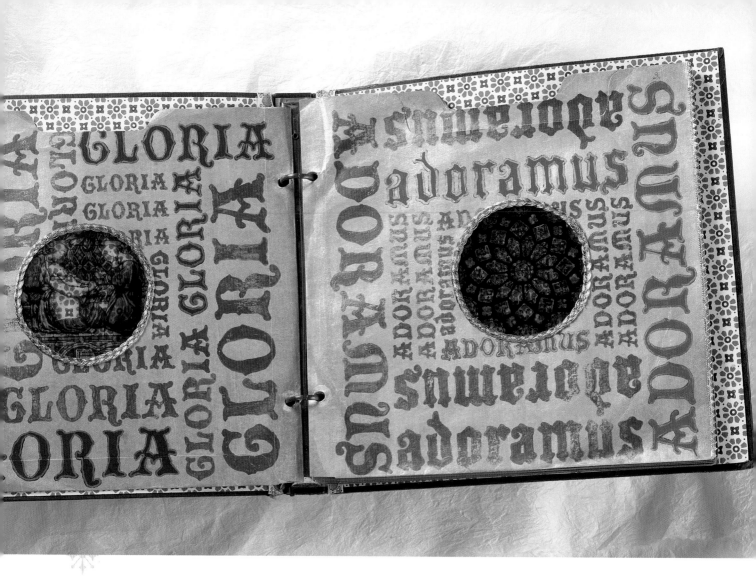

The pockets that once held vinyl records in this notebook album are given subtle brilliance with a ground of sheer gold acrylic paint. Repetitive use of hand painted text resounds with beautiful praises to God.

1 Brush archival paper paste onto the back of a patterned paper and apply it to the front of the vintage LP album. Smooth out any small paste bubbles by running your hand across the cover with light pressure. Repeat this treatment on the back cover.

2 Use a contrasting paper (the one featured is a bronze, leather-textured paper) to wrap the binding edge on the left. Adhere with an archival paper paste brushed onto the back of the paper.

3 Using the gold metallic paint pen, select imagery in the patterned paper to highlight or illuminate by tracing around desired forms or letters.

4 Line the inside of the album covers (both front and back) with a different patterned paper using the same technique employed in step 1.

5 Adhere decorative jacquard trim atop the liner paper on the inside cover adjacent to the album's rings.

6 Lightly dry brush a thin coat of sheer acrylic metallic gold paint over each of the album's pages. Set aside to dry. While your piece is drying, begin creating a basic text design by first sketching it on a piece of paper the same size as the vintage album's insert. Alternatively, a basic text design can be created on the computer using computer fonts and then printed out. Either way, remember to account for the hole in the album pages when creating your design concept.

7 Now that your design is finished, lay a sheet of carbon transfer paper (carbon side down) on top of one of the gilt album pages. Next, place your design sheet (created in step 6) on top of the carbon paper. (Taping these sheets in place with drafting tape will help minimize error and shifts in the design.)

8 Begin tracing all the text by outlining your design with a pencil, ballpoint pen, or ball-tipped burnishing tool. When all the text has been outlined, lift up your design sheet and transfer paper. Your text art design will now be transferred to the album page.

9 Choose three words from the text design that you will accentuate by painting with acrylic paint. Allow to dry thoroughly.

10 Use the fine-tipped, gold metallic paint pen to outline the painted letters for an illuminated look.

11 Use the same gold metallic paint pen to fill in all the remaining words on the page.

12 Place a photo or print of a stained glass window inside the pocket where the vinyl record would have been stored. (The images featured here are manufactured on transparency material and help add to the window illusion.) The hole where the record's label would show through will perfectly frame your image. Adhere into place.

13 Finish the piece by adhering German gold foil paper borders or other metallic gimp and trim to the edge of the page. Use the same or coordinating trim to finish the hole that features the stained glass print.

LEFT Each of the pocket pages has a hole where the record label was once visible. Now that void is the fitting place for inspiring imagery of cathedral stained glass windows. To enhance the window inference, the stained glass imagery used here is a semi-translucent transparency material.

BELOW A sleek little CD book has a chic cover decked out in scrapbook embellishments and fashion detailing such as machine stitching. The piece features music that caters to the soul and a design that caters to the style conscious.

Soul Music
CD BOOK

MATERIALS

cardboard CD case
  (manufactured or recycled)
CD
patterned paper
patterned transparency
chipboard letters and metal
  letters
wood flower, epoxy stickers,
  and various scrapbook
  embellishments
rub-on letters
decorative ribbon
hook and loop tape
  (Velcro)

TOOLS

acrylic paint
brush
metal adhesive
sewing machine
paper awl

ARTIST: *Julie Scattaregia*

FOR MANY PEOPLE OF FAITH, WORSHIPPING GOD IS associated with modern praise music. Singing these songs to honor the Lord elevates the participants to a place of adoration for God and what He has done in their lives. The style of worship can vary, but whether it is with bended knee, bowed head, or lifted hands, the end result is the same: a heart of exaltation and praise. The same is true for an artful faith book or journal: no matter what the style of execution, a paper-crafted book of worship can escort your soul to God's presence and focus your mind on God and God alone. The embellished CD book showcased here is a place to both stow away a CD of a favorite, cherished praise song (or collection of them), and also to record reflections on what the praise music has meant to your faith in a mini booklet residing alongside the CD. Together the elements of this worship book form a volume to nurture one's soul.

"Sing to the Lord a new song; sing to the Lord, all the earth."
PSALM 96:1

1 Remove the black snap-in holder for the CD. Do not be overly concerned about any natural tearing that may occur in the cardboard surface, as it will be covered over in subsequent steps.

2 Adhere patterned paper to the front, back, and interior panels of the CD book.

3 Machine sew squares of transparency to the front and back covers using a zigzag stitch along the perimeter.

4 Paint chipboard letters to coordinate with the patterned papers.

5 Tie bows around a select few chipboard letters with the decorative ribbon. (Here the "M" and "I" are given this detail.)

6 Adhere the chipboard letters and complement with other metal letters and scrapbook embellishments to spell out the title and fill out the cover design. (Be mindful to use the appropriate adhesive when bonding metal to paper.) Use a paper awl to pierce the cardboard where any decorative brads are used.

7 Adhere a pre-manufactured booklet to the left interior panel. The booklet featured here has a transparency cover to coordinate with the transparency art sewn to the CD book's cover.

BELOW A purchased and embellished mini booklet secured on the left conceals private introspection about worship. On the right, rub-on letters spell out a worshipful expression (that is also a line from the song on the CD) directly onto the disc's surface.

8 Reattach the black snap-in CD holder to the right panel with adhesive. Laying a heavy book or other object on it as it dries overnight will help ensure a secure bond.

9 Using rub-on letters, create a title on the CD itself, mimicking the circular shape of the disc.

10 Center and adhere a small piece of hook and loop tape on the ends of the interior right and left panels to create a closure.

*"Surely the righteous shall give thanks to Your name;
The upright shall dwell in Your presence."*

PSALM 140:13

Folding Stencil
SCREENS

ARTIST: *Sharon Soneff*

MATERIALS

letter stencils
  (in three different sizes)
patterned papers
  *(flocked, metallic, and
  handmade)*
decorative gimp trim
metallic jacquard ribbon
gold metallic spray paint
gold leaf size
gold leaf flakes
black cardstock
craft hinges
  *(two hinges between
  each letter)*

TOOLS

metal adhesive
hot glue gun
brush
  (small, flat-bristled)

SOMETIMES IN A BUSY LIFE OF TASKS AND OBLIGATIONS, pausing to give God worship is easily forgotten. However, a decorative reminder placed prominently in view can be just the prompt to take us out of our earthly mindset and into one more heavenly focused. A small altar or triptych, or even a simple folding screen such as those presented in this project, will serve both as an artifact of beauty and a piece to stir thoughts of God and His goodness. The screen project begins with basic letter stencils in three sizes, which are then enhanced by a coat of metallic gold spray paint. The stencils are lent further texture and richness with a refined application of gold leaf around the negative space that forms each letter character. Splendid papers (some flocked, some handmade) paired with opulent trims complete the panels that are then hinged together to spell out names of God. One glance at these magnificent screens will inspire contemplation of things more divine.

1 Choose letters from the stencil pack to spell out the desired name. The stencils come with the inner portion of the letters perforated but intact. Punch out the negative space of the letters and discard.

2 Lay out the letters on newspaper and spray the faces with metallic gold spray paint. Allow paint to dry.

3 Prepare the stencil cards for a second treatment of gold by sparingly brushing on gold leaf size to the inner edges of the letters on each card. Allow to dry for about one hour, or until the size becomes tacky.

4 Press the gold leaf flakes onto the inner edges of the letters. The flakes will hold where the sizing was brushed on. Brush away the excess flakes.

5 Apply adhesive to the back of each card (either by running through an adhesive transfer machine or by hand applying a paper crafting paste with a brush). Then lay patterned paper (decorative side up) on the back of each letter stencil card (so that the pattern is showing through the negative space of the letter stencil). Trim off any excess patterned paper.

6 Mount each card on a larger piece of black cardstock.

7 Using the hot glue gun, adhere decorative trim around the perimeter of each letter.

8 Line the cards up in order face down and position two hinges between each letter panel. Using the appropriate adhesive for affixing metal to paper, attach each hinge to the screen back.

9 Place screen upright and zigzag the panels back and forth so the piece is stable.

LEFT Gold leaf furthers the theme of texture and opulence. Judiciously applied, the leaf is a delicate detail that smartens the screen's whole appearance. Here, paper with flocked, velvetlike designs makes the letter character even more sumptuous.

GALLERY

ABOVE A chunky album is jammed full of artful content. Wrapped up with a glitzy bow, the book beckons to be opened and reveal the surprise pages within it.

Praise His Name
FOLD-OUT BOOK

ARTIST: *Sharon Soneff*

An origami-like fold-out album is the optimum platform for exhibiting a large collection of photos or memories in one spot. The collection displayed in this fold-out book, however, is just a small sampling of the many worshipful names for God found in the Bible. Each of the thirty panels is given a unique treatment of regal papers and trim to exhibit expressions of God's character and deity. When the book is unfolded and spread open, the multiple panels (sixteen panels on one side and fourteen panels on the flip side) instantly encourage worship. The names illustrated in the book can be meditated upon and even prayed aloud in adulation. Each square is a decorative moniker eliciting a tone of reverence and honor to the very nature of who God is.

ABOVE Unique letter treatments combined with a special selection of papers and embellishments characterize each of the names of God. The use of German Dresden gold foil letters, computer fonts, and a range of scrapbook stickers helps to accomplish the distinct executions.

BELOW The succinct album opens to reveal a surprisingly large and diverse assemblage of names and characteristics of God. With thirty distinct panels, the complete album is a visual banquet.

"Let them praise the name of the Lord: for His name alone is excellent; His glory is above the earth and heaven."

PSALM 148:13

ABOVE Sparkly red glitter and gleaming gold leaf finish off the collage treatment on this Latin choral hymnal's cover. Secured with a satin bow, the hymnal is converted from a songbook of worship to an art piece of worship.

Illuminated
HYMNAL

ARTIST: *Jennifer Hardy Williams*

WITH MYSTERIOUS LAYERS AND RICH symbolism, the art of collage illumines the content of the Latin hymns in this book. Layer upon layer of torn papers dress the hymnal's cover with a texture that invites closer inspection. Fold-out attachments created from translucent vellum provide a panorama of images and type to reverberate the worshipful messages in the hymns. The torn splices of scripture incorporated into the fold-out scene validate and enlighten these age-old canticles. An exquisite use of glitter, leafing, and velvet and satin ribbons makes this hymnal enigmatic and beautiful.

ABOVE With strong visual metaphors, the art on this fold-out scene further illustrates the material of the hymn. Here the imagery and text shed light on the "Agnus Dei" hymn, reminding us of Jesus's great sacrifice for us.

BELOW Glorious glittered birds resound the theme of the "Adoramus" hymn as do the scriptures pieced atop this vellum fold-out panel. Here the art dutifully inspires and enlightens.

"Therefore, by Him let us continually offer the sacrifice of praise to God, that is, the fruit of our lips, giving thanks to His name."

HEBREWS 13:15

BELOW This vintage church hymnal has a warm, old-fashioned appeal with fabric strips dressing the spine and tabbing meaningful hymns within. The cover is fashioned on the computer, then printed out and adhered to the hymn's existing cover. A top glaze of gel medium lends protection and beauty.

"Let the word of Christ dwell in you richly in all wisdom, teaching and admonishing one another in psalms and hymns and spiritual songs, singing with grace in your hearts to the Lord."

COLOSSIANS 3:16

Then Sings My Soul
ALTERED HYMNAL

ARTIST: *Deb Perry*

LOCATED IN THE BACK OF EVERY PEW IN MOST traditional churches are the familiar hymnals reached for every Sunday to lead congregations in unanimous anthems. For many, attached to these songs are vivid memories of a loved one, such as a father or grandmother. Stories of their faith, and how it has been passed down over the generations, have strong links to these honored old songs. An old retired hymnal provides the perfect backdrop to record such stories of previous generations, artistically documented for generations to come. Altered with fabric remnants, charms, transparencies, paint, and photographs, the piece is then finished with handwritten journaling and personal sentiments. This altered hymnal is transformed from a common songbook to a priceless family heirloom and a truly unusual kind of scrapbook.

ABOVE The black floral framework on each page is printed onto transparencies, sewn to a paper base, and then adhered to the hymnal's page. The fabric remnant theme is repeated here, but in a new way: they become leaves sewn into the composition. Handwritten journaling and personal photos lend a scrapbook appeal to this altered hymnal where memories abound.

RIGHT Hymns of special significance are tabbed with a fabric remnant sewn to the edge. A swash of color provided by acrylic paint is used to frame the hymn and point to key phrases.

LEFT A bold use of color and form makes a dynamic statement on this large art journal. Hand lettering and a playful mix of pattern and color make this cover unconventional and fun.

RIGHT A photo enlargement acts as the ground for this page. Swatches of patterned papers are casually arrayed directly on top of the photo, where the face and form are enhanced by penned outlines.

Worship Together Forever
JUMBO ART JOURNAL

ARTIST: *Elsie Flannigan*

ACRYLIC PAINTS, INK, SNIPS OF PATTERNED papers, and playful photos become the offering of worship in this jumbo journal. Sweet thoughts toward God are hand penned on snips of paper and layered over an exuberant mix of mediums. To accomplish the grand scale that virtually shouts honor to God, the artistic elements of this book go jumbo. From the giant, vibrant painted heart on the cover to large paper flowers applied to pages within to the even bigger photos, everything about this book says, "My God is big and so is my love for Him!" Modern and contemporary, this art journal displays that a passion for Christ is never out of style.

LEFT A radiating flower crafted from scrapbook paper complements the happy tone exuded by the photos and the funky hand-lettered statement praising God.

ABOVE Sweet statements about God's beauty are lightheartedly scrawled on regular notepad paper. When the edges are inked and the paper is applied to this bohemian mix of patterns, the result is far from regular.

"Every day will I bless Thee; and I will praise Thy name for ever and ever."

PSALM 145:2

BELOW Diminutive in scale but grand in presence, these small dioramas elaborately detail scenes where the forms of nature and mankind exist to give God enjoyment and pleasure.

The World is the Theatre of God's Glory.

Gloria Patri.

"For it is God who is at work in you, both to will and to work for His good pleasure."

PHILIPPIANS 2:13

Theatres for
HIS PLEASURE

ARTIST: *Jennifer Hardy Williams*

KNOWING OUR EXISTENCE AND DAILY ACTIVI-ties are both purposed and delighted in by our Heavenly Father gives our everyday pursuits value and meaning. A quote from John Calvin, French reformer and theologian, speaks to this precept and provides the central theme for this dimensional worship piece. "The world is the theatre for God's glory" is declared on the glittered, furling banner above the assembled cast of sweet characters cut from vintage photos and ephemera. These two magnificent theatres begin as ordinary boxes that are placed on their sides. Openings are sliced into the lids to design a space for an embellished scene. Paper crafted trees, sparkling rhinestones, showy gold stars, silver and gold leafing, tulle, and *ribbonerie* all add to the dazzling stage for the delightful performers.

ABOVE In a separate smaller box, a vintage photo of two children in costume is centered within a cartouche frame.

RIGHT Delicate cardstock branches and punched maple leaves are lent stability when adhered to an undetectable base of clear acetate. Minute details, such as the crystals encrusting the banner and the gold stars rising above it, bestow intricate beauty to this theatre.

Chapter 3
SCRIPTURE BOOKS

Introduction by Mindy Caliguire

A perennial problem of spiritual life is this: forgetfulness. We simply forget. We forget that God exists, that He is trustworthy, that He forgives and heals and restores. We forget and lose perspective. We forget and lose hope. We forget and lose kindness. We forget and lose peace. We forget and lose our way. Thankfully, we are intimately known and loved in the midst of our amnesia! God chose to reveal himself in several of the most powerful communication vehicles available—through the beauty of nature; through the person of his son, Jesus; and in the penetrating power of a book. A compilation of words. Letters. The Holy Scriptures.

Composed of sixty-six different books, authored by roughly forty different people, and written over the course of nearly 1,500 years, the Bible records the compelling story of God at work through human history. We read of the ordinary and extraordinary lives of people just like us—prone to wander, apt to fail, eager to find meaning and purpose, hungry for truth and life and justice and peace. Ordinary people. Extraordinary words. The Bible reveals God as One who is deeply concerned with the condition of human life and willing to employ drastic means to bring us the kind of hope, restoration, and peace we most need.

The sad truth is that for too many of us, the life-changing, life-giving message of the Bible remains tucked between dark pages, never to see the light of day. Never to bless the lives of the very people for whom it was written.

And yet we so desperately need to hear these words of life! To be reminded, often, of the very things that can build trust and help us remember what this life is all about. And then life gets busy and we invariably miss the joy, the peace, and the hope so readily available to us in a relationship with God.

Long stretches of reading and reflection on the writings of scripture can refresh and rejuvenate you. But even excerpts can feed the soul. "For the Word of God is living and active…" (Hebrews 4:12a) Depend on it. And then surround yourself with words of life in artistic and captivating ways. You have every reason to expect you will sense the activity of God.

"By your words, I can see where I'm going…"

PSALM 119:105 (THE MESSAGE)

BELOW Rich hues and materials are married together in a book whose shape reveals its theme: *God's Heart*.

God's Heart BOOK

MATERIALS

fine art paper
  (Stonehenge)
acrylic paint
gel medium
black rub-on letters and numbers
tissue paper and/or sewing
  patterns
black India ink
stamping Ink
fabric remnants
thread
ribbon
foil

TOOLS

calligraphy pen and nibs
rubber stamps
scissors
paintbrush
awl
sewing machine

ARTIST: *Christine Adolph*

ONE OF THE MANY DIVERSE PURPOSES OF THE HOLY Scriptures is to reveal God's character to us so that we can know Him more intimately and form a relationship with Him. One artist's pursuit to know the heart of God through scripture was realized in a book whose literal shape was inspired by the theme. A hand bound book with heart-shaped pages is the platform for multiple mediums framing hand-inked scriptures. The calligraphic handwriting is interspersed with swash styled, rub-on capital letters and numbers, creating added flair. Featured on radiant mediums of foil and iridescence, each of the scriptures acclaims God's unconditional, everlasting love for His people. This synthesis of art and scripture is wholly elevating.

"Behold what manner of love the Father has bestowed on us, that we should be called children of God!"

I JOHN 3:1A

Psalm 33
11 and 13-15

But the plans of the Lord stand firm forever, the purposes of his Heart through all generations

From heaven the Lord looks down and sees all mankind; from his dwelling place he watches all who live on earth he who forms the Hearts of all

1. Cut eight to ten large hearts out of the fine art paper.

2. Using gel medium, collage the tissue paper and/or sewing patterns to the front and back of each of the paper hearts. Allow to dry.

3. Brush a wash of acrylic paint on each of the collaged heart surfaces (front and back) to form a foundation for other mediums.

4. Using a sewing machine, stitch around the perimeter of each of the heart shapes with a zigzag stitch.

5. Fold each of the hearts in half and crease.

6. Unfold all the hearts and lay them flat. Using an awl, punch two holes in the center fold of each heart, duplicating the same hole position on all the hearts.

7. Stack the hearts on top of one another and lace a ribbon through the holes, finishing with a bow on the spine edge.

8. Embellish the cover with blocks of fabric, stitching, painting, and stamping. Create a title with rub-on letters.

9. Create entries for the interior heart pages by first rendering the scripture reference with a combination of rub-ons and hand lettering written with the calligraphy pen and nibs in India ink. (The beginning capital letter shown is a rub-on with hand lettering in the text that follows.)

10. Continue to embellish the heart pages by surrounding the scriptures with stamped patterns, pen and ink illustrations, acrylic paint, and fabric blocks.

OPPOSITE When opened up, the book's full heart pages display hand-inked scriptures that are surrounded by illustrations and stamped patterns in bright and brilliant mediums.

BELOW Luminous and lovely, the entries in this heart journal are scriptures that reveal God's love and purpose to His children.

BELOW A compact, spiral-bound book of coin envelopes splashed with a trio of modern colors makes a utilitarian yet stylish place to stow a collection of favorite verses from the book of Proverbs.

Envelope
BOOK OF PROVERBS

ARTIST: *Sharon Soneff*

A COMPACT VOLUME OF WISDOM IS FOUND IN THIS compendium of Proverbs where scriptures are housed in small, brightly painted coin envelopes. Smart coordination of color and function is the central design statement of this project. God's Word is intended to offer applicable wisdom to our everyday lives, and this book offers a place to store some of it. The bound collection of envelopes is well suited to serve as the repository for a surplus of scripture verses. Tucked inside each envelope is a scripture that can be used for personal enrichment or to share and encourage another. Small details like mini brads, velvet ribbon, and a library plate, all in highly contrasting black, show nicely against the vibrant color provided by paint and patterned paper. Bound together by a black spiral and enclosed with colored elastic, the piece becomes a concise source of scriptures.

MATERIALS

manufactured envelope
  spiral book *(7 Gypsies)*
OR
twelve small coin envelopes and
  chipboard covers spiral bound
  at your local copy store
black mini brads
black library plate
patterned paper
cardstock
  *(in three colors pulled from the
  palette of the patterned paper)*
black velvet ribbon
colored fashion hair elastic
three coordinating colors of
  acrylic paint

TOOLS

mini punch
awl
paintbrush
paper adhesive
hot glue gun
scissors

"My son, if you receive my words, and treasure my commands within you, so that you incline your ear to wisdom, and apply your heart to understanding."

PROVERBS 2:1–2

BELOW With a smart use of type, scriptures and their references are printed out on cardstock to match the paint color of the corresponding coin envelope.

1 Disassemble the components of the spiral book, taking the cover and envelopes off the spiral binding.

2 Paint the front and back chipboard covers with acrylic paint, being mindful to paint all the edges. Set aside to dry.

3 Adhere the patterned paper to the faces of the chipboard pieces. (Note: leave the spine area uncovered, with the coat of paint exposed. Leave the reverse sides of the chipboard uncovered, with the paint treatment showing.)

Trust in the Lord with all your heart, & lean not on your own understanding.

Proverbs 3:5

4 Create a label to go behind the library plate on the colored cardstock. The label here was created in photo editing software, but it can just as easily be created in a word processing software or by hand.

5 Attach the library plate to the cover by first piercing the cardstock label with an awl and attaching the library plate to the cardstock label with matching mini brads. Then adhere the finished plate to the cover with a hot glue gun.

6 Paint each of the coin envelopes, using a rotation of three different colors taken from the palette of the patterned paper on the cover.

7 Adhere the same patterned paper that was used on the cover to the front of each of the coin envelope's flaps. Then punch a small hole in the center of the point of the flap and attach a mini brad. Now adhere the patterned paper to the rear of the flap disguising the splayed prongs of the brad.

8 Print (or hand write) one scripture on each piece of colored cardstock. Adhere a black velvet tab to the back of each card by folding a small piece of velvet ribbon and hot gluing in place. This tab will allow you to easily remove the scripture from its coin envelope.

9 Reassemble the book by threading the front cover, the coin envelopes, and the back cover back onto the spiral binding.

10 Create a closure for the book by stretching a colored hair elastic across the center of the book. This aides in keeping the book neat and confined since the bulk of material would otherwise make the book unmanageable.

ABOVE Finished with a black velvet ribbon tab, the scripture card can easily be extracted from the coin envelope that encases it.

deb

Seeking One

WHEN MY HEART WHISPERED,
"SEEK GOD,"
MY WHOLE BEING REPLIED,
"I'M SEEKING HIM!"

PSALM 27:8

grant

Generous Heart

WHEN DARKNESS OVERTAKES THE
GODLY, LIGHT WILL COME
BURSTING IN. THEY ARE GENEROUS
COMPASSIONATE AND RIGHTEOUS.

PSALM 112:4

morgen

Abundant Provider

LET YOUR LIGHT SO SHINE
BEFORE MEN THAT THEY MAY SEE
YOUR MORAL EXCELLENCE, YOUR
NOBLE AND GOOD DEEDS AND
PRAISE YOUR FATHER WHO IS IN HEAVEN.

MATTHEW 5:16

mason

Strong One

BUT AS FOR ME,
I AM FILLED WITH POWER,
WITH THE SPIRIT OF THE LORD,
AND WITH JUSTICE AND MIGHT.

MICAH 3:8

lindsae

Refreshing One

THE LORD, YOUR GOD, ... WILL REJOICE
OVER YOU WITH GLADNESS. WITH
HIS LOVE, HE WILL CALM ALL YOUR
FEARS. HE WILL EXULT OVER YOU BY
SINGING A HAPPY SONG.

ZEPHANIAH 3:17

ABOVE A grouping of plaques, one for each family member, is an impressive exhibit of color, type, and design, as well an impressive exhibit of scripture.

Scriptural NAME PLAQUES

ARTIST: *Deb Perry*

MATERIALS

8" × 10" (20.3 × 25.4 cm)
  stretched canvas
white cardstock
fabric remnants
fabric ribbon
copper wire
glass beads
charms

TOOLS

decoupage medium
sandpaper or steel wool
staple gun
hot glue gun

BIBLICAL SCRIPTURES ALSO OFFER ENCOURAGEMENT and blessings to believers. One artist personalized the blessing of scripture by creating canvas plaques that fuse textiles, wire, beads, type, and imagery to work in accord with the name, its meaning, and the personality of each family member. Joined together by common attributes such as distressed typographic frames, wire accents, and consistent fonts, the pieces feel like a family when grouped together. But they are distinctly different too, as each plaque bears colors and themes that specifically reflect each member as an individual. Each name is expressed in bold-faced serifs, and the unique meaning of the name is articulated below it in an antiquelike script. Grounding it all is a specially chosen scripture presented in all capital letters that reverberates the meaning with a blessing from the Bible.

"A good name is to be chosen rather than great riches, loving favor rather than silver and gold."

PROVERBS 22:1

THE LORD, YOUR GOD, ... Y
OVER YOU WITH GLADN
HIS LOVE, HE WILL CAL
FEARS, HE WILL EXULT O

A handmade wire form is threaded with beads and charms that specifically reflect the personality and talents of the person for whom the plaque was created.

1 Take a fabric remnant and stretch it over the face of the canvas, securing it with a staple gun to the wooden frame on the back.

2 Adhere a length of patterned ribbon to the perimeter edge of the canvas using a hot glue gun.

3 Create the content of text and imagery on your computer and print onto heavy white cardstock. Tear the edges of the cardstock to reveal a raw white edge.

4 Adhere the cardstock to the fabric base using decoupage medium. Allow to dry.

5 Further distress the edges of the cardstock by lightly sanding the surface using fine sandpaper or steel wool. Seal the surface with two thin coats of the decoupage medium, allowing it to dry between coats.

6 Wrap the perimeter of the canvas with copper wire. (Note: In some cases, the wire was wrapped around the wood frame and canvas by piercing the canvas with an awl and slipping the wire in and out of the pierced holes.) Loop and knot the wire (as with a bow), slipping coordinating glass beads and charms onto the loops randomly as you proceed.

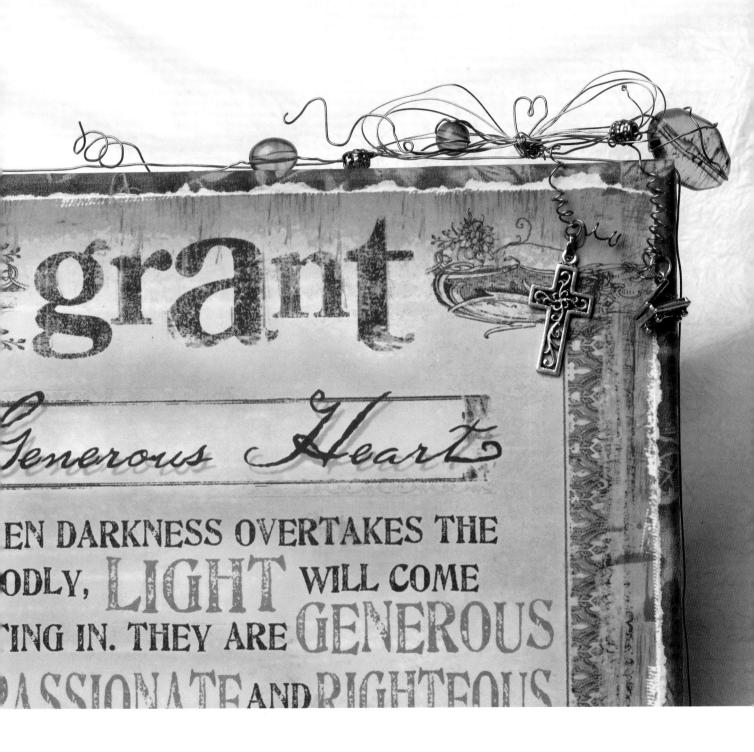

grant

Generous Heart

EN DARKNESS OVERTAKES THE
ODLY, LIGHT WILL COME
ING IN. THEY ARE GENEROUS
ASSIONATE AND RIGHTEOUS

GALLERY

ABOVE A quartet of collaged boxes becomes a regal place to nest a collection of vintage, palm-sized testaments.

LEFT Florid and fanciful, these boxes treat the scriptures that lie in repose like prized treasures.

Nested
TESTAMENT BOXES

ARTIST: *Jennifer Hardy Williams*

LIKE TREASURE BOXES THAT ARE FILLED WITH invaluable riches, these handsomely collaged boxes do *indeed* house invaluable riches: Holy Scriptures. Nesting within each box is a palm-sized vintage *Old* or *New Testament*. Gold foiling, regal wax seals, and rich wide satin ribbon all infer the richness of the boxes' contents. While these artistic devices express the worth of the scriptures, the labels atop each box further express it through Biblical excerpts explaining the purpose and value of God's written word. Every surface, from edge to inner lid, is thoughtfully adorned. A rare combination of scripted papers and floral motifs is accented by an assortment of butterfly imagery. These exceptional scripture boxes make a deserving place of distinction for the Bible.

ABOVE Inscribed on a label atop each box is a handwritten Bible verse that emphasizes the importance and preciousness of the scriptures that rest within.

RIGHT The existing embossed detail on the vintage leather testament cover lends an opportunity for a traditional gold leaf treatment.

"For where your treasure is, there will your heart be also."

LUKE 12:34

RIGHT The walnut ink-stained cover of this accordion book lends a classic appeal, while the pastel blue enamel heart buckle laced with rickrack and a peek of a ribbon's edge are the only hint of what lies within.

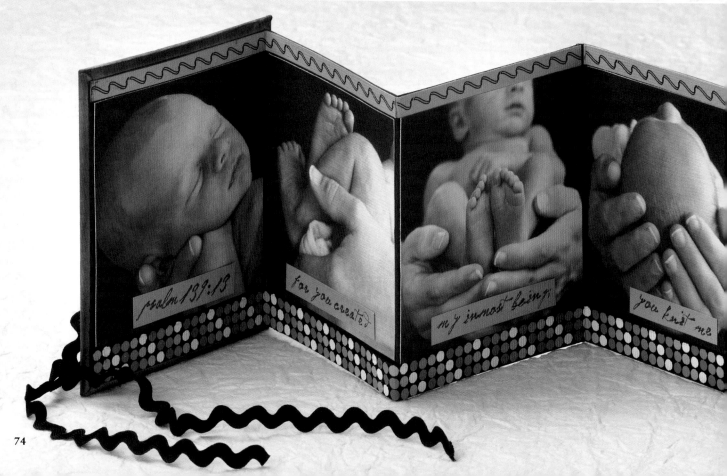

Photographic
ACCORDION BOOK

ARTIST: *Melissa Diekema*

Sometimes one Bible verse can be such a poignant revelation from God. In this accordion book, a single verse spans its entire length, running across a panoramic sequence of exceptional black-and-white newborn baby photos. Yet that one verse here does so much more than act as an ordinary caption for the photos; rather, it infuses them with great meaning and significance. Minimal but carefully chosen trim and embellishments complement rather than compete with the photos and verse. Nothing detracts from what is of primary importance: the newborn baby and God's words about such a child. This project wholly exemplifies how finding a scripture that speaks directly to the subject matter of your photos can result in a stunning end product.

"All scripture is given by inspiration of God…"

II TIMOTHY 3:16A

ABOVE Choice details, like printing the photos on textured cardstock and bordering the piece with graphic ribbon, make this book sophisticated and polished.

BELOW An incredible sampling from a photographer's shoot of a precious newborn baby becomes the focal point for a fold-out album where scripture serves to amplify the subject matter.

BELOW With jubilant color and whimsical forms, the scripture featured here is the artist's favorite passage regarding the qualities of a virtuous woman; embellishing her own photo with paper wings and a crown, the artist playfully expresses the way she feels in Christ.

acter who can find? She is worth far more than rubies. and works with eager hands... She provides food for nsiders a field and buys it; out of her earnings d. She sets about her work vigorously: is profitable, and her lamp does not She opens her and extends eedy. When it snows ettold; for all of them makes coverings fore... d purple...She makes linen peaks with wisdom... many surpass them... d beauty man who ised...

PROVERBS 31

Our Favorite Scriptures
TABBED BOOK

ARTIST: *Elsie Flannigan*

A TABBED MINI BOOK PROVIDES A CREATIVE space for a couple's favorite scriptures to dwell. Each tab indexes one such favorite scriptural excerpt, where it is archived for future reference and inspiration. Photos that enliven the Bible verses allow this scripture book to double as a scrapbook of sorts. Biblical passages are written out by hand, and the irregular characteristics of the handwriting are precisely what impart the perfectly imperfect properties of the book's overall playful design. And a profuse use of color and pattern make this animated record of scriptures considerably more fun to refer to than a stiff concordance.

"But whoever keeps His word, truly the love of God is perfected in him. By this we know that we are in Him."

I JOHN 2:5

TOP Clippings from patterned paper punctuate the scripture and create accents to the adjacent photo; the scripture featured is from the couple's wedding ceremony, so their casually romantic photo (topped with a jumbo monogram symbolizing their shared last name as man and wife) seems particularly apropos.

ABOVE Here, the paper snippets take on graphic forms as a more masculine rendering of pattern lends the backdrop to the husband's favorite scripture.

RIGHT A file-folder style mini book is the underpinning of a collection of favorite scriptures for a young married couple. Simple paper scraps and ribbon remnants show an artful and resourceful use of material that is nothing short of sensational.

TOP This slender stack of papers is full of both visual and spiritual inspiration.

BOTTOM Pivoting from a single post, the pages of this swatch book can fan out for a fun display of its contents.

Happiness
FAN DECK

ARTIST: *Beth Wilkinson*

A FAN DECK APPROACH TO THIS PROJECT GIVES it originality. The content of the scriptures that speak to finding happiness gives it spiritual value. Sparkling crystal studs and rhinestone brads add to the already joyful tone. And when all the pages are swiveled out from the post, it becomes a rainbow of promises from God's Word in bright art and type. This artist's exploration reveals yet another purpose of scripture: to cheer the spirit and instill joy in one's soul.

LEFT Spelled out in fashionable fonts and happy colors, the scriptures are further accessorized by sparkling crystals, rhinestones, and trim.

BELOW The message of the Bible verses, joined with a playful use of type, form, color, and materials, results in a finished piece that is positively uplifting.

"I will delight myself in thy statutes: I will not forget thy word."

P S A L M   1 1 9 : 1 6

Ordination

31. July 2005

Chapter 4
SPIRITUAL EVENTS

Introduction by Mindy Caliguire

Days seem to come in varying lengths, though they all contain the same twenty-four short hours. Some days just fly by! Others crawl past at a snail's pace. One thing is for sure: whether we race or crawl through our days, time marches on. Even as you read this, the second-hand is ticking, ticking, ticking. Time goes by in only one direction; it is immovable, irrevocable, and eventually, gone.

Amid the swiftly moving days, some stand out in stark contrast. These days etch themselves into our personal histories—not to be swiftly forgotten like sand castles left at the edge of the incoming tide, lost to the advancing waves of time.

Some days stand out because they change us forever. We risk losing touch with a critical part of our identity should we forget their transforming impact upon us. Of course, we never intend to forget…but we do.

The writer of this ancient psalm asks God to help him "number his days" in order to gain a heart of wisdom. It seems like an odd idea. What does it mean? We number our days when we see the value of each one. We gain wisdom when we are aware of the significance of our days. And we especially gain wisdom when we identify and cherish those days which marked our lives forever.

This chapter invites you to do just that. Commemorate the days in your life (or in a loved one's life) that have been significant spiritually. On the following pages, you'll find several ideas for highlighting and creatively recording those significant events.

As you create beautiful pieces to commemorate the life-defining events that occurred on otherwise ordinary days, you'll be more apt to remember them. And the wisdom gained will be yours to keep.

"Teach me to number my days, that I may gain a heart of wisdom."

PSALM 90:12

TOP The tackle box provides a delightful and unusual place for spiritual histories to be stowed. A scripture about being fishers of men is a clever tie-in to the theme.

BOTTOM A series of embellished file folders rests in the tackle box's bottom compartment; each file folder is a mini scrapbook with unique testimonies found inside.

Vintage Tackle Box of
SALVATION STORIES

ARTIST: *Deb Perry*

THE SINGLE MOST PIVOTAL EVENT IN MOST CHRISTIANS' lives is the day of their salvation prayer, but few Christians can actually remember the details of that event, and even more rare are those who have created anything to commemorate it. Here, a 1920s tackle box holds these invaluable stories of the salvation experience as remembered by the artist and her family members. The top tray is filled with vintage fishing lures, each with an attached alphabet charm bearing the initial of the family member whose salvation story can also be found in the box. Below the top tray is a bottom compartment where upright file folders contain the details of the artist's interviews with her family members. When the dialogue of these interviews is documented scrapbook style with photos, patterned papers, stamps, and embellishments, the result is a prized heirloom chronicling the spiritual heritage of this family for generations to come.

MATERIALS

tackle box
fishing lures
alphabet charms
ribbons
craft wire and/or jump rings
cross charm
white rub-on letters
alphabet stickers
quilting fabric remnant
linen tape
cardstock
patterned paper
thread
miscellaneous scrapbook
  embellishments

TOOLS

gel medium
opaque pens
stamps
stamping ink
scissors
craft pliers
paintbrush
corner rounder
sewing machine

"And he will speak words to you by which you will be saved, you and all your household."

ACTS 11:14

ABOVE When the lid is opened, an inscription rendered on quilting fabric in white opaque ink and white rub-on letters makes the purpose of the box more evident.

1 Clean and prime the areas of the tackle box where paper or fabric will be applied.

2 Adhere patterned papers to flat paneled areas of the exterior faces of the tackle box. A combination of whole pieces and torn strips of patterned paper was used here for artful texture. (Note: Even the latches on this particular box provided flat areas where the papers could be used.)

3 Further enhance the lid with scriptures or typography, either written by hand or using letter stickers.

4 Create an aged appearance by rubbing a sepia brown ink sparingly on the paper surfaces (particularly the paper edges).

5 Seal the patterned paper surfaces with matte gel medium.

6 Attach an array of lengths of ribbons to the tackle box handle. Add a charm to the center of the handle with a wire or jump ring.

7 Adhere the quilting fabric remnant on the interior of the lid and in the top tray. Finish with linen tape.

8 Using a white opaque pen and/or white rub-ons, create a title or inscription in the lid to identify the contents or purpose of the box.

9 Attach alphabet charms (signifying the names of the people whose stories the box will hold) to the fishing lures using wire or jump rings. Lay them loosely in the top tray.

10 To create file folders, score and fold cardstock laterally and finish the corners with a paper rounder. (Alternatively, manufactured file folders can be modified to fit.) Cover with patterned papers and create a tab by attaching a cardstock square. Add an alphabet sticker or die cut to the square, showing the initial of the person whose salvation story will be relayed on the file folder.

11 Handwrite or type the interview on a piece of paper that will be adhered to the interior of the file folder.

12 Adorn the interior of the file folder with photos, stamping, sewing, painting, or any other embellishments.

BELOW Using an interview style to document family salvation stories and a scrapbooklike execution to communicate them, the artist gathers a collection of file folders that holds a legacy of faith.

ABOVE One major benefit to handcrafting an album is the ability to designate unique shapes for the cover and pages.

Cross-Shaped
HAITI BOOK

ARTIST: *Julie Scattaregia*

EVEN SHORT-TERM TRIPS OF SERVICE ABROAD CAN LEAVE lifelong fingerprints on one's memory. Therefore, crafting a momentous album for the photos and impressions of such a mission trip seems only proper. Long after a return to home soil, the reflections and emotions connected to a missionary trip can be conjured and shared through a book that artfully records them. A cross-shaped album as featured here is an atypical presentation of one artist's missionary trip to Haiti. Joined together by loose-leaf rings, chipboard covers and cardstock pages bear embellishments and papers that are illustrative of the revival experience on the island.

MATERIALS

chipboard sheet
chipboard letter
patterned papers
rub-on letters
loose-leaf rings
bead ball chain
large, decorative eyelets
decorative brads
staples
silk flowers
ribbons
printed twill
charms
cardstock
metal-rimmed tags
paper clips
  ("owl style")
stamping ink

TOOLS

hole punch
eyelet setter
paintbrush
adhesive
scissors
stapler
foam or rubber stamps
  *(alphabet set and another
  with large icon or motif)*

"Go therefore and make disciples of all the nations, baptizing them in the name of the Father and the Son and the Holy Spirit."

MATTHEW 28:19

"The humble will be filled with fresh joy from the Lord. Those who are poor will rejoice in the Holy One of Israel."

ISAIAH 29:12

LEFT The distinctive shape of the album allows for pages with unique composition that are far more dynamic than the usual rectangular pages of a typical book.

1 Cut two identical cross shapes from chipboard material.

2 Adhere patterned paper to the crosses and trim to the edge of the chipboard.

3 Create a dozen or more interior pages from cardstock, duplicating the shape of the chipboard cover.

4 Punch two holes at the top of the cross-shaped chipboard cover. Mark the position of these holes onto the back chipboard cover and punch again. Then duplicate this process with all the interior pages.

5 Attach decorative eyelets into the holes of the covers.

6 Add two loose-leaf rings, feeding them through the top holes of the front cover, the interior pages, and the back cover.

7 Adorn the loose-leaf rings by attaching ribbons. Loop a small bead ball chain through one of the rings to attach a charm and tags.

8 Using foam or rubber alphabet stamps, stamp the title of the album onto the cover, leaving out one or more of the letters. Replace the missing letters with a chip-board letter.

9 Using a large icon stamp, stamp a motif randomly two or three times on the cover.

10 Staple a piece of printed twill to the cover.

11 Pierce the center of a single silk flower blossom with a decorative brad and attach to the chipboard cover.

12 Proceed by covering interior pages with patterned papers and photos. Use metalrimmed tags attached to the pages by owl clips to create captions.

GALLERY

ABOVE Hue, textural material, pattern, and type are used to impart the destination and culture of the artist's missionary trip.

Mission to China
ALBUM

ARTIST: *Beth Wilkinson*

THE BEAUTIFUL ETHNICITY OF THE PEOPLE seen and served on this artist's missionary trip is mirrored in the design elements she created for her memory album. From the Chinese red hue of the cover and pages, to the embossed and engraved charms and brads that accent them, the cultural flavor of the missionary trip is tastefully manifested. The modest, spiral-bound book that is the base for the project can hardly be detected when the spine is covered and layered with strips of printed typographic elements and woven Maruyama paper. Further use of typographic elements, built graphically to embrace favorite photos of the trip, add to the rich allure.

ABOVE The title page, designed and printed on the computer, is enhanced with dimensional items such as an old Asian coin and patterned index tabs.

RIGHT Entry pages feature single photos of the missionary trip framed by typographic ornamentation and supplemented by decorative brads and charms. This project is a wonderful example of how to successfully blend the handcrafted and digital arts.

"As cold waters to a thirsty soul, so is good news from a far country."

PROVERBS 25:25

Nathan's Dedication
SHADOW BOX

ARTIST: *Jennifer Hardy Williams*

THE VERY FIRST SPIRITUAL EVENTS OF OUR lives often occur when we are but tiny infants. While we may not remember them, the prayers and commitment that culminate in a baby's dedication ceremony are still an important part of our spiritual timeline. This artist's son will not remember his dedication service, yet this engaging shadow box commemorates it in a way that honors the event prominently in the home and will let him know what importance the family places on a commitment to Christ. With a hinged glass front door protecting the elements beneath, the shadow box holds an array of literal and symbolic pieces that are fixed and pinned to the upholstered back, creating a stunning montage of the event.

LEFT Complex layering of emblematic materials, pierced by gleaming pearl-topped pins, are winsome elements in the display case.

OPPOSITE A glass-front shadow box gives prominent appointment to the mementos of a baby's first important spiritual event.

"Train up a child in the way he should go; and when he is old, he will not depart from it."

PROVERBS 22:6

Wedding
CANVAS

ARTIST: *Elsie Flannigan*

WHILE MANY VIEW A WEDDING AS A HUGE social affair, the event is really more about the sacred and holy vow before God than it is about the dress, the flowers, and the catering. Here an artist pays tribute to her wedding day while revering the union as a spiritual one and not simply a ceremonial one. Her wedding day photo is flanked by collaged components where the love the couple shares is attributed to its source: the love bestowed on them by Christ. Phone book pages cut into lovebird shapes are just a portion of the entire collaged scene bursting with love and passion.

LEFT Paint-covered phone book pages and buttons are part of the unexpected collage composition honoring the matrimonial spiritual event.

OPPOSITE A canvas washed with bold strokes of red acrylic paint is the base for a collaged art piece expressing the spiritual significance of a wedding.

"Therefore shall a man leave his father and his mother, and shall cleave unto his wife: and they shall be one flesh."

GENESIS 2:24

BELOW A sparse but choice use of lovely materials on this page allows the stirring photo to become the primary focus. Scriptures printed on ink-jet transparency make a sleek and elegant presentation communicating the event's Biblical significance.

And all who have been united with Christ in baptism have been made like him.

Galatians 3:27

Come to the Water
BAPTISM ALBUM

ARTIST: *Sharon Soneff*

A BAPTISM CEREMONY IS ANOTHER MILESTONE spiritual event common to the experience of many believers. While the baptism ceremony itself differs among various churches and denominations, the basic purpose is the same: an outward profession of faith. For many Christians, baptism marks a new level of growth and empowerment in their spiritual walk, so it seems fitting that this event be acknowledged in an album of its own. This album's cover and pages take cues from the seaside setting where this baptism was performed; the colors, textures, and elements of the beach make a beautiful background and foreground to the photos featured in the middle ground. A repetitive use of clear beads threaded on twisted wire alludes to the water element present in baptism. Glass glitter, sea glass, and shells further develop the theme. And finally, a sublime use of blue embroidered and handmade papers beautifully emphasizes the deep azure ripples in the sea.

LEFT A rectangular window cut in the interleaving tissue of the manufactured album allows the baptism photo to peek through. Additionally, a dove shape is cut from highly glittered paper; then small lengths of beaded, twisted wire are attached, radiating from behind the paper dove to the top of the photo.

TOP LEFT An album focused on a baptism conducted in the waters of the ocean is given seaside-influenced ornamentation. Beaded wire, studded with actual shells, frames the central photo and spine of a gray linen album.

"He who believes and is baptized will be saved..."

MARK 16:16

For Christ did not send me to baptize but to preach the gospel, and not with words of eloquent wisdom, lest the cross of Christ be emptied of its power. For the word of the cross is folly to those who are perishing, but to us who are being saved it is the power of God.

1 Corinthians 1: 17–18

LEFT The first spread in the album features the invitation for the ordination service, where a brass bookplate on the opposing page highlights key words in scripture relevant to the event.

ABOVE A sophisticated use of black and white papers makes this a handsome album to recognize a significant pastoral event.

Ordination
MEMORY BOOK

ARTIST: *Jennifer Hardy Williams*

In an artful show of support of her husband's ordination into pastoral ministry, this artist combines refined papers, exquisite transparencies, translucent vellum, and stitched ribbon into a memory book fitting this landmark in the couple's spiritual life. Emphasizing her husband's love of scripture and theological studies that led to his ordination, the album is heavily layered with scriptures and type. A discriminating palette of black, white, and gray highlighted by warm brass hardware and golden-hued, scripted papers lends to the profound, stirring feel of the piece. Stately and dignified, the memory book combines beauty, function, and meaning under one cover.

ABOVE Decoratively printed transparency and sheer printed vellum are combined to make a stunning title page that overlays a key photo of the event.

RIGHT More photos of the event help to capture the powerful nature of the service. Metal index tabs add more than mere utility when housing compelling scripture references.

"And how shall they preach, except they be sent? As it is written, How beautiful are the feet of them that preach the gospel of peace, and bring glad tidings of good things!"

ROMANS 10:15

The fruit of the spirit is love joy peace patience kindness goodness gentleness faithfulness and self-control.

galations 5:22-23

LOVE

thankful thankful grateful
grateful thankful
thankful grateful grateful thankful

& I lay down my life for the sheep

Psalm 34

It's so amazing to me that something written by a man hundreds of years ago can effect me so much. But it does... it inspires me encourages me, admonishes me. And that's a good thing. I have dedicated this book to the thoughts I have while reading this book by David... how I can apply it to my life, what my feelings are when I read each individual verse, and how it encourages me in my everyday walk as a Christian...

(All scripture taken from the King James Version)

Chapter 5
BIBLE STUDIES

Introduction by Mindy Caliguire

One of the surest ways to deepen your experience of God is to share the journey with companions; fellow travelers who share the same desire for God and for His purposes. Soul friends, you could call them. In fact, those kinds of relationships were intended to be a primary source of life and growth.

You may wonder why bringing others into your private spiritual journey would be so beneficial. Well, there are numerous reasons: some people appreciate the accountability of loving friends who ask hard and well-aimed questions. Others find a smaller group setting simply more conducive to spiritual learning than a large worship service or teaching. Still others might enjoy time to pray together, an opportunity to discuss personal points of application, or the ability to receive encouragement from those who know them well.

If you have the pleasure of experiencing spiritual growth in a community with friends or family, this chapter offers numerous ways to energize the creative juices of the group. What have you learned together? How could you represent that learning artistically?

Far from being selfish or self-centered, when we share our stories in light of what God has done and is continuing to do in our lives, we model the actions of the psalm below: we do not hide what we have learned or received. We do not conceal His love and faithfulness. We share it. And when we do, everyone benefits and God is honored.

However, you really don't need a great assembly—or even a mini-assembly. It may be that your faith book on a particular Bible study is a very solitary act. But in recording your reflections and insights so beautifully, you inadvertently invite others to share in what you gained. Others will want to see, read, and consider what you express in a project based on Bible study. As you share your story, you honor and bless the One who is the ultimate author of your life.

"I do not hide your righteousness in my heart; I speak of your faithfulness and your saving help. I do not conceal your love and faithfulness from the great assembly."

PSALM 40:10

ABOVE A stainless steel board with interchangeable parts becomes an interactive hub for a family's study of the fruits of the spirit.

Got Fruit?
STAINLESS BOARD

ARTIST: *Deb Perry*

MATERIALS

stainless steel sheet
metal primer
patterned papers
chipboard letters
magnets
clear plastic pocket
small spiral-topped notebook
large die-cut letters
epoxy letter stickers
metal and paper decorative
  borders
gum or candy tin
rickrack
thread
cardstock stickers and die cuts
decorative hook
bulldog clip
stamping ink

TOOLS

paintbrush
metal adhesive
scissors
sewing machine

Utilizing materials commonly used in scrapbooking, this artist transforms a sheet of stainless steel into a focal point for putting into practice a family Bible study on the fruits of the spirit. The metal backdrop allows the magnetic pieces and pockets to be changed to reflect different fruits of the spirit as the family progresses in their study from month to month. One month the focus might be love, while the next month the focus might shift to joy or peace or patience; all that needs to be done to reflect the subject change is to switch out the magnetic letters and the card in the pocket to designate and define the fruit being studied. As the family applies what they've learned, they make an entry into the notebook on the hook, documenting how they are evidencing the fruits of the spirit in their everyday lives. As the notebook is filled up, it can also be exchanged for a new one. This practical, hands-on approach to studying the Bible as a family couldn't be more fun.

"I am the vine, you are the branches. He who abides in Me, and I in him, bears much fruit; for without Me you can do nothing."

JOHN 15:5

1 Clean and prime the stainless steel sheet to receive the paper.

2 Using adhesive for paper to metal applications, apply the patterned paper to the board. (Note: Three different papers were used here, with the primary paper in the center and the two complementing papers trimming out the top and bottom sections of the board.)

3 Rub sepia or brown ink directly on the paper edges to create an aged effect.

4 Trim the seams where the patterned papers meet the metal and paper borders.

galations 5:22-23

LOVE

meeting another's needs unselfishly.

as we study the fruit of the spirit, take time to notice them in each of our lives. When you do, grab a pen and "record the evidence" in this little notebook. I love to watch God at work in your lives!
mom

evidence of **LOVE** dec. 2, 05

"Mom, take all the money you were going to spend on me and give it to Paige and Madison for Christmas so that they will have presents to open."

— what Lindsae said to me when I asked for her christmas list.

5 Type a scripture pertaining to your Bible study subject matter (Galatians 5:22–23 shown for the Fruits of the Spirit study) and print out on cardstock. Cut out each individual word of the print out and ink the edges. Adhere to the top two-thirds of the stainless board in an irregular fashion.

6 Attach a decorative hook to the open upper right area of the stainless board with a bulldog clip.

7 Cover the spiral top notebook with patterned papers, cardstock stickers, and die cuts. (Here "Evidence 4 the Record" is conveyed in scrapbook stickers.) Thread rickrack trim through the spiral spine and knot the slack at the top. Hang the notebook on the hook.

8 Adhere the clear pocket to the central portion of the board (positioning it below the Bible verse and to the left of the hanging notebook). Place a series of cards in the pocket, bearing the name and definition of an element of the study. Embellish with stickers, patterned paper, rub-on decorations, and/or machine stitching.

9 In the lower portion of the board, adhere a metal photo frame. In the center of the frame, place epoxy alphabet stickers (here they spell out "got"). Now adhere jumbo die-cut patterned paper letters atop the frame and along the expanse of the bottom of the board (here they spell out "fruit?").

10 Adhere magnets to the back of chipboard letters that will be placed on the steel board to spell out the subject being studied. Spare letters for the other subjects being studied in other months are stored in a gum or candy tin.

ABOVE The homey mix of patterns lends the warmth and appeal of a country quilt. Vintage fruit stickers and die-cut images emphasize the theme and add to the whimsy.

GALLERY

BELOW Unique expressions of the individuals who fashioned them, these mini composition books provide a place to record and reflect upon revelations learned during a group Bible study on the subject of gratitude and thanksgiving.

Gratitude COMPOSITION BOOKS

ARTIST: *Julie Scattaregia*   *with Wendy Barnes, Trish Bentivoglio, Lindy Keers, Julie Pells, Valerie Salmon, and Terri Sanford*

WHEN ONE ARTIST GATHERED A GROUP OF women together to scour the Bible for its truths on gratitude, she added a creative element. By furnishing each member of the study group with an ordinary mini composition book and a trove of scrapbook papers and supplies, she amplified the entire experience. The distinctive approaches to covering and embellishing the composition books reveal the differing vantages on the subject. Not only does the craft of adorning the book allow for one kind of expression, but the book itself becomes a platform for another type of expression: written notes and entries within. Facilitated by the lead artist, the participants came away from the project enriched by the scriptural study and by discovering gifts of creativity they didn't realize they had.

LEFT Internal entries further expound upon the theme of thankfulness established in the Bible study group and expressed on the books' varied covers. The process of creating causes the participants to dig deeper, look inward, and contribute in a fresh way.

"And let the peace that comes from Christ rule in your hearts. For as members of one body you are all called to live in peace. And always be thankful."

COLOSSIANS 3:15

BELOW Once unfinished and bare, now transformed into art pieces, these crosses display a group of artists' responses to meditating on and studying the Passion of Christ.

So it is no longer I who live, but it is Christ who lives in me. This life that I live now, I live by faith in the Son of God, who loved me and gave his life for me. ~ Galatians 2:20

love

blessed

Pardon, Peace and Power

That's my King!

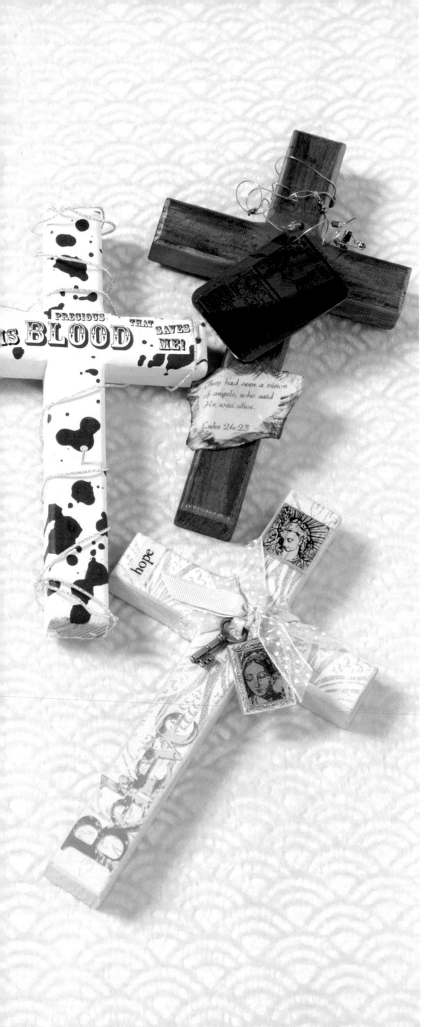

Cross
BIBLE STUDY

ARTIST: *Sharon Soneff*
with Susan Schaeffer, Beth Wilkinson,
Eric Wilkinson, and Julie Williford

WHAT COULD OTHERWISE BE A SOMBER BIBLE
study on the heavy subject matter of the cross
becomes more enlivened and personal as
the artists involved express their impressions
of the study through art. Each participant,
having been supplied with only a bare
wooden cross, alters it into a metamorphic
manifestation of what the cross means to
them as an individual. The wide-ranging
designs generated by the group demonstrates
how distinct and personal the experience was
for the participating artists.

"For to this end Christ both died,
and rose, and revived, that he might
be Lord both of the dead and living."

ROMANS 14:9

GALLERY

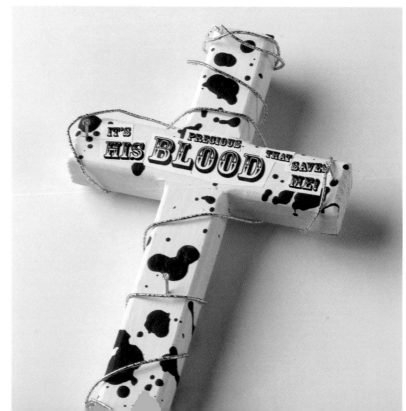

ABOVE Metaphoric materials speak volumes on a small surface. From fine gauge wire that forms a heavenly filament above one cross to the red Swarovski crystals judiciously placed on the other, the messages lie in the small details.

OPPOSITE BOTTOM A vivid interpretation of the cross by one artist is provocative, powerful, and poignant. The venture of availing the arts in a Bible study setting in and of itself incorporates emotion.

ABOVE Compelling imagery laden with significance, paired with intriguing technique, evidence the absorbing nature of the topic in the materialization of the crosses.

"I have been crucified with Christ; it is no longer I who live, but Christ lives in me; and the life which I now live in the flesh I live by faith in the Son of God, who loved me and gave Himself for me."

GALATIANS 2:20

ABOVE A ransom letter approach to the title of this circle journal makes a colorful and quaint proclamation. Torn edges and unfinished threads lend a wonderfully raw feel.

RIGHT Rolled pages from vintage devotionals and homilies add texture and discreet messages pertinent to the Bible study on God being our shepherd.

Shepherd Me
CIRCLE JOURNAL

ARTIST: *Jennifer Hardy Williams and Dale R. Williams*   *with Sharon Soneff and Beth Wilkinson*

WHEN A QUINTESSENTIAL CIRCLE (OR ROUND-robin) journal is organized around the ancillary purpose of studying the Bible, the creative experience is augmented by a spiritual one. The lead artist who fashioned this marvelous journal enlisted her partici-pants to contemplate what it means for God to be our shepherd through a meditation on the twenty-third Psalm. The artist's husband, who is also a seminarian and reverend, was an added asset and inspiration to all who were involved. The journal was mailed cross-country, and each participating artist added a skin of paper, paint, ephemera, and candid journaling to the base structure beneath. When it was returned to the lead artist, the book was filled with an artful and exhaustive look at Psalm 23.

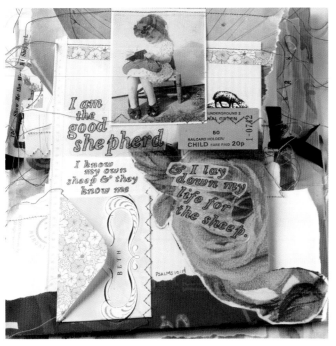

TOP Green hues, reminiscent of a grassy pasture, are used by one artist. In a gracious use of old and new, a vintage engraving and a hymnal leaf are also employed to execute the entry.

LEFT With an urban bohemian flair, another artist accom-plishes her entry with a mix of varied patterns, type, imagery, and eclectic materials.

"The Lord is my shepherd; I have everything I need."

PSALM 23:1

GALLERY

ABOVE The combined efforts of two artists in one journal reflect their desire to be vulnerable and accountable to one another while pursuing the beauty that is found in Christ.

RIGHT The artists spur each other on, posing questions to one another and themselves. Statements of faith and devotion in a whimsical hand are scattered amongst dried flowers, angelic photos, and lace.

Beauty Is Vulnerable
JOURNAL

ARTIST: *Elsie Flannigan and Rachel Denbow*

TWO YOUNG ARTISTS TRANSLATE THE PURSUIT of scripture and the quest for real beauty into a shared journal that is passed between them. Pages layered with scriptures studied, scribbles and illustrations, self portrait photos, and revealing inner thoughts all contribute to a journal that gets increasingly more layered as the artists continue to exchange the book with one another. The juxtaposition of raw elements such as torn masking tape with more formal elements such as lace and hymnal pages makes visually captivating pages. The multilayered, multitextural sum of their artful efforts becomes a creative journal of real substance.

ABOVE One provoking aspect of the artists' Bible study is the way they paraphrase scriptures in a form that is meaningful and personal to them. The artists' drawings and annotations have the intimate quality of a private diary.

RIGHT A total abandonment for Christ and the Holy Scriptures is undeniable; clearly depicting this are photos of the artists exhibiting their unrestrained zeal for life and the God who has blessed them with it.

"And let the beauty of the Lord our God be upon us, And establish the work of our hands for us; Yes, establish the work of our hands."

PSALM 90:17

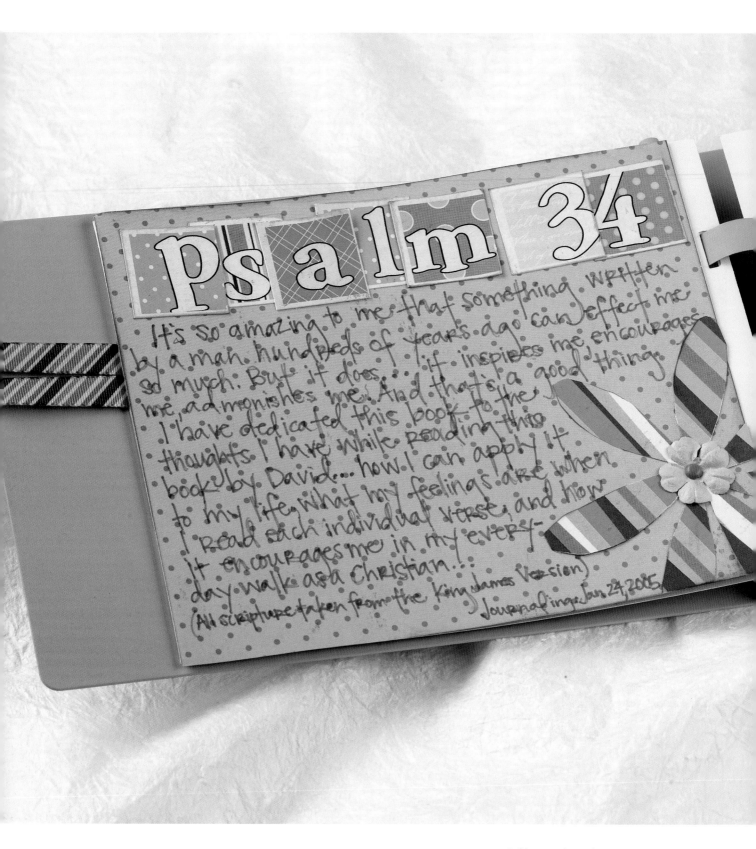

Psalm 34

It's so amazing to me that something written by a man hundreds of years ago can effect me so much. But it does.... it inspires me encourages me, admonishes me. And that's a good thing. I have dedicated this book to the thoughts I have while reading this book by David.... how I can apply it to my life, what my feelings are when I read each individual verse, and how it encourages me in my every-day walk as a Christian....

(All scripture taken from the King James Version)

Journaling: Jan 24, 2005

ABOVE A title page shows the artist's close examination of one chapter in the Bible and identifies her emotions and discoveries about an ancient book in a contemporary world.

Psalm 34 Up Close and Personal
METAL ALBUM

ARTIST: *Cheryl S. Manz*

One method of studying the Bible is a straightforward chapter-by-chapter, verse-by-verse survey. Whether done singly or in a group, this simple strategy for looking at scripture can still be invigorating. Creating a vibrant volume for the dissection of scripture is the first step; here one artist shows us precisely how that can be done. A clear-cut format that invites, rather than intimidates, is another aid in successfully carrying out an in-depth, on-going exploration of the Bible. The spirited and vivacious color and embellishment of the album calls the artist to come and dive into the Word of God as an act of joyous spiritual enrichment.

ABOVE A hinged, metal album with adornments in hot colors assures that this independent Bible study will be neither stale nor dry.

RIGHT The left-facing page of every spread in the album isolates one verse of the chapter being analyzed. The right-facing page of every spread responds to the adjacent verse with honesty, transparency, and relevancy.

"Study to shew thyself approved unto God, a workman that needeth not to be ashamed, rightly dividing the word of truth."

II TIMOTHY 2:15

GALLERY

RESOURCES

3M
www.3M.com
Transparencies, laminating
supplies, and adhesives

7 GYPSIES
www.7gypsies.com
Scrapbook paper and
embellishments

AC MOORE
www.acmoore.com
Art and craft supplies

ALL MY MEMORIES
www.allmymemories.com
Paper, ribbon, and other
scrapbook supplies

ALPHA STAMPS
www.alphastamps.com
Gift wrap, rubber stamps,
collage supplies

ALTERED PAGES
www.alteredpages.com
Ephemera products, scrapbook
and collage supplies

AMERICAN CRAFTS
www.americancrafts.com
Paper, vellum, embellishments,
pens, markers, and cards

ANNA GRIFFIN, INC.
www.annagriffin.com
Decorative paper and
embellishments

ARTCHIX
www.artchixstudio.com
Vintage images, rubber stamps,
transparencies, paper, and
embellishments

ARTCITY
www.artcity.com
Art and craft supplies, frames,
and furniture

ARIZONA ART SUPPLY
www.arizonaartsupply.com
Art supplies

AUTUMN LEAVES
www.autumnleaves.com
Scrapbook paper, books, and
embellishments

AVERY
www.avery.com
Tags, labels, and office supplies

BASICGREY
www.basicgrey.com
Cutting-edge decorative papers

BAZZILL
www.bazzillbasics.com
Cardstock

CAPTURED ELEMENTS
www.capturedelements.com
Decorative papers

CAROLEE'S CREATIONS
www.caroleescreations.com
Decorative paper and
embellishments

CHATTERBOX
www.chatterboxinc.com
Scrapbook paper and
embellishments

CREATIVE IMAGINATION
www.cigift.com
Decorative paper, supplies, and
embellishments

DAISY DS
www.daisydspaper.com
Decorative paper

DELTA
www.deltacrafts.com
Acrylic paint and craft supplies

DESIGN ORIGINALS
www.d-originals.com
Scrapbook paper, supplies, and
embellishments

DICK BLICK ART MATERIALS
www.dickblick.com
Art supplies

DMC
www.dmc.com
Embroidery thread and other
fibers

EK SUCCESS
www.eksuccess.com
Patterned paper, supplies, and
embellishments

FIBERS BY THE YARD
www.fbty.com
Fiber, twill, ribbon, and trim

FISKARS
www.fiskars.com
Scissors, deckle-edge scissors, and
other cutting tools

FONTWERKS
www.fontwerks.com
Paper, ribbon, and rubber stamps

FOUND ELEMENTS
www.foundelements.com
Vintage items, ephemera,
and collage supplies

FUNKY FIBERS
www.funkyfibers.com
Wholesale only–fibers by
the yard

GLUE DOTS INTERNATIONAL
www.gluedotsinternational.com
Adhesive dots for paper craft
applications

GOLDEN ARTIST COLORS
www.goldenpaints.com
Colors, gel mediums, gessos,
gels, grounds, and varnishes

GRAFIX
www.grafixarts.com
Plastic films and decorative products

HEIDI SWAPP
www.heidiswapp.com
Scrapbook and paper-crafting
products

HERO ARTS
www.heroarts.com
Art stamps

HOBBY LOBBY
www.hobbylobby.com
Craft supplies

JACQUARD
www.jacquardproducts.com
Paints and pearlescent powders

JO-ANN FABRIC & CRAFTS
www.joann.com
Fabric, scrapbook, and craft supplies

JUDIKINS
www.judikins.com
Rubber stamps, supplies, and
Diamond Glaze

KI MEMORIES
www.kimemories.com
Scrapbook paper, supplies, and
embellishments

K&COMPANY
www.kandcompany.com
Scrapbook paper, albums, and
embellishments

KAREN FOSTER DESIGN
www.karenfosterdesign.com
Scrapbook paper, stickers, and
embellishments

KOLO
www.kolo.com
Albums, scrapbooks, presentation
binders, and storage boxes

KREINIK MANUFACTURING
www.kreinik.com
Threads, beads, and fiber

KRYLON
www.krylon.com
Spray and brush-on paints and
finishes

LAZAR STUDIOWERX
www.lazarstudiowerx.com
Decorative papers, die cuts,
rub-ons, fiber, and stamps

LI'L DAVIS
www.lildavisdesigns.com
Scrapbook paper, supplies, and
embellishments

LIQUITEX
www.liquitex.com
Paint and craft finishes

LOERSCH CORP.
www.loersch.com
Slide mounts, frames, and tools

MAGIC SCRAPS
www.magicscraps.com
Scrapbook embellishments and
supplies

MAKING MEMORIES
www.makingmemories.com
Scrapbook paper, tools, supplies,
and embellishments

MANTO FEV
www.mantofev.com
Collage and assemblage art supplies

MARVY UCHIDA
www.uchida.com
Markers, ink, and hole punches

MAY ARTS
www.mayarts.com
Ribbon

MAYA ROAD
www.mayaroad.com
Ribbon, fiber, stickers, and
embellishments

MELISSA FRANCES
www.melissafrances.com
Labels, paper, frames, tags, and
transfers

MICHAEL'S
www.michaels.com
Art and craft supplies

MY MIND'S EYE
www.mymindseyeinc.com
Scrapbook paper, die-cut alpha-
bets and frames, rub-ons, and
stickers

OFFICE DEPOT
www.officedepot.com
Office supplies

OFFRAY
www.offray.com
Ribbon

PAPER ADDICT
www.paperaddict.com
Scrapbook paper

PAPER SOURCE
www.paper-source.com
Flat paper and stationery, rubber
stamps, book-binding supplies,
journals, and albums

PAPER STYLE
www.paperstyle.com
Scrapbook supplies, invitations,
and stationery

PAPIER VALISE
www.papiervalise.com
Mixed-media supplies

PEARL PAINT
www.pearlpaint.com
Art supplies

PLAID
www.plaidenterprises.com
Acrylic paint, stamps, paper, and
tools

PRESSED PETALS
www.pressedpetals.com
Pressed flowers, stickers, paper,
vellum, and tags

PRISM
www.prismpapers.com
Fine cardstock

PROVO CRAFT
www.provocraft.com
Cutting systems and tools, paper, stickers, embellishments, and albums

RANGER
www.rangerink.com
Ink, ink pads, and related products

REX ART
www.rexart.com
Art supplies

RUBBER STAMPEDE
www.rubberstampede.com
Rubber stamps and art stamps

RUSTY PICKLE
homepage.mac.com/rustypickle
Albums, hardware, ink, leather, lace, paper, ribbon, stamps, stickers, and tags

SEI
www.shopsei.com
Scrapbook paper, stickers, die cuts, iron-ons, embellishments, and albums

SAKURA
www.sakura.com
Archival pens and markers

SANFORD
www.sanford.com
Sharpie markers

SCRAP ARTIST
www.scrapartist.com
Digital kits, digital papers, digital embellishments, and community

SCRAPWORKS
www.scrapworks.com
Scrapbook paper, tools, supplies, and embellishments

SCENIC ROUTE PAPER
www.scenicroutepaper.com
Scrapbook paper, stickers, die cuts, and embellishments

STAMPINGTON & COMPANY
www.stampington.com
Rubber stamp and collage art supplies

STAPLES
www.staples.com
Scrapbook papers and albums, office supplies

STICKERS GALORE
www.stickersgalore.com
Stickers

TARGET
www.target.com
Home accessories and stationery supplies

THERM O WEB
www.thermoweb.com
Adhesives

TWO PEAS IN A BUCKET
www.twopeasinabucket.com
Scrapbook supplies, fonts, digital kits, ideas, and community

X-ACTO
www.hunt-corp.com
Knives and blades

XYRON, INC.
www.xyron.com
Adhesive application machines, cutting and printing tools

WALNUT HOLLOW
www.walnuthollow.com
Wood embellishments

WESTRIM
www.westrimcrafts.com
Scrapbook and paper-art embellishments

CONTRIBUTING ARTISTS

Christine Adolph

Christine Adolph is an artist who uses combinations of mixed-media floral collage, surface pattern design and illustration, foil imaging, collage, paint, and drawing with acrylics and watercolors in most of her design and artwork. She licenses her work for the gift, home decor, and craft markets. She has designed six lines of stamps for Stampington & Co., and her products, by Creative Imaginations, include numerous collections of scrapbook paper and embellishments. Her work has appeared in many national publications, including *Legacy; Somerset Studio;* and *Cloth, Paper, Scissors.* Books featuring her work include *Pockets, Pullouts, and Hiding Places* by Jenn Mason; *Beyond Scrapbooks* by Barbara Bourassa; and *Making Family Journals: Projects and Ideas for Sharing and Recording Memories Together* by Linda Blinn. She lives in southern California with her husband and two daughters.
www.christineadolph.com

Rachel Denbow

Rachel Denbow can't go a week without getting paint on her clothes. She uses her sewing machine, leather tools, paints, and forgotten objects to create a variety of redesigned or original pieces. These include handbound leather journals, funky aprons, large personal art journals, and smaller starter journals full of whimsy for others to make their own. Rachel is part of Red Velvet Art, a design group that creates products for girls and offers classes on how to make a beautiful mess. She is currently working on an art journal with Elsie Flannigan to document their growth through transition and long distance phone calls. Rachel lives with her husband in Seattle, Washington, and is starting a baby line inspired by the bump in her belly.
redvelvetart@hotmail.com

Melissa Diekema

Melissa Diekema is a long time scrapbooker and lover of photography. She is on the design team for Fontwerks and does freelance writing for *Better Homes and Gardens* and *Scrapbooks, Etc.,* as well as having her work featured in the magazines in various forms. She started a photography business in 2005 and enjoys candid photography of people of all ages. An avid runner, she spends much of her time keeping up with her three children. She lives with her husband, Paul, and their children in Michigan, where you will find them enjoying the beach during the summer and complaining about the cold during the winter.
www.melissadiekemaphotography.com

Elsie Flannigan

Elsie Flannigan is an artist at heart. She loves to combine her passions for art, photography, and preserving memories into meaningful family scrapbooks. She is a frequent contributor to *Creating Keepsakes Magazine,* a Garden Girl design team member for www.twopeasinabucket.com, a stamp designer for Fontwerks, and a member of the KI Memories Design Team. For fun, she loves to decorate her home, make jewelry, and watch films. Elsie is also a member of Red Velvet Art (www.redvelvetart.com), an art group passionate about creating from within and expressing your true self. She lives in Springfield, Missouri, with her husband, T.J., and their pug, Cocoa. You can catch up with her at her blog, **www.elsieflannigan.blogspot.com.**

Cheryl S. Manz

Cheryl Manz is currently going to graphic design school and is working toward the hope of one day having her own line of scrapbook products. She has been scrapbooking for almost six years and has been published more than 200 times. Her style is very bright, colorful, and alive as she tries to express her gratitude for life in her pages. She is currently on the design teams for Scenic Route Paper Company, American Crafts, and *Scrapbook Answers Magazine.* Cheryl travels often to scrapbook conventions to teach others new innovative ideas. **www.cherylmanz.typepad.com**

Deb Perry

Coming from a background of fine art and graphic design for over twenty-five years, Deb Perry ventured on to the scrapbooking scene in November of 2003 at the urging of her sister-in-law. Creating with an eclectic mix of layers and bold graphic design, she works in both digital and paper mediums, often combining both into the same project. Deb is published regularly in the magazines and idea books of *Memory Makers* and *Creating Keepsakes,* and her layouts were recently published on the covers of *Simple Scrapbooks Digital Four* and *Creating Keepsakes.* Earning Top 20 honors for Memory Makers Masters was a first in 2004, and in 2005 she was chosen Top 50 in the *Creating Keepsakes* Hall of Fame Contest. She also creates for several manufacturer design teams and recently finished her first collaborative book project. Whether she is designing with a gel pen or her Wacom Digital Tablet, Deb loves the art of handwriting and drawing, so her layouts typically include this free-form element. When not scrapbooking, she enjoys homeschooling, photography, fine art drawing, watercolors, and taking mini vacations with her husband and three teens. **www.scrapbookresumes.com**

Julie Scattaregia

Julie was introduced to scrapbooking shortly after the adoption of her first child eight years ago. She's been passionate about it ever since. In 2003, Julie was inducted into the *Creating Keepsakes* Hall of Fame. She has since authored Creative Imagination's premier idea book, *Your Sentiments Exactly.* Julie has also recently written two additional CI books, *Totally Transparent* and *The Sports Page.* Her designs have been featured in several scrapbook magazines and idea books. A former corporate trainer, Julie loves to share her creativity by teaching scrapbook classes. She has been a Creating Keepsakes University instructor for the past three years and also loves to teach in her hometown. Along with instructing, Julie designs for some fun and innovative scrapbook product manufacturers. Julie lives in Carmel, Indiana with her husband, Steve, her two beautiful children, Alexa and Aidan, and one Vizsla dog, Abby. Her family is the love of her life and her motivation for scrapbooking, providing her with endless creative inspiration. **scrappyscat@aol.com**

Susan Schaeffer

Susan is passionate about all art-related endeavors, first and foremost scrapbooking, collage, and creating unique rubber-stamped cards and gifts. She has a degree in business and by day works as a court reporter. Susan credits such books as Julia Cameron's *The Artist's Way* for balancing her life between work and pursuing her art and craft interests. Susan is pleased she is able to nurture the creative artistic spirit in her daughter and son. She lives in Long Beach, California, with her husband and two children.

Beth Wilkinson

Beth Wilkinson has had a love for creativity and art since she was a child. She studied fine art and graphic design in college. This launched her into the world of commercial art, where she picked up her diverse knowledge in marketing and the fashion industry. From this vast background comes her fresh vision for vivid colors and stylistic illustrations. She has since entered the scrap- booking industry, designing products and brand development for Sonnets Studios. Beth lives in southern California with her husband and a son on the way. **beth@sonnetsstudios.com**

Eric Wilkinson

Eric Wilkinson has a background in fine art, graphic design, and illustration. He enjoys sharing his love of art with children, teaching youth art classes. He is also involved in commercial endeavors with his art. He has a passion for drawing, illustration, and three-dimensional art. Eric lives in southern California with his wife and a son on the way. **eric.wilkinson@cox.net**

Julie Williford

Julie draws artistic inspiration from the great masterpieces of painting, sculpture, architecture, and nature she has seen and studied throughout Europe. She enjoys creating one-of-a-kind rubber-stamped cards and gifts with an Old World flavor and utilizing antique photography in her creations. Julie has a degree in history and a master's in business finance and keeps her computer humming throughout the day with her work as a financial analyst. She stays connected to her creative side through her treasured relationships with gifted women such as Sharon and Susan. Julie lives in Newport Coast, California, with her two boys, who rejuvenate her spirit daily.

Dale R. Williams

Dale R. Williams hold a Masters of Divinity from Westminster Seminary California in Escondido and is an ordained pastor in the Vineyard Association of Churches. His contribution to this book represents his very first endeavor as an artist. He is currently working at Baker Academic, a Christian publishing house in Michigan, and is enrolled in the Masters of Theology program at Calvin Seminary in Michigan. When Dale is not hard at work, he can be found surfing the Great Lakes. Dale lives in Michigan with his wife, Jennifer, their son, Nathan, and three pesky, crazy cats. **http://logeia.blogspot.com**

Jennifer Hardy Williams

Jennifer Hardy Williams is an assistant professor of English Literature at Calvin College in Michigan. Mixed-media art and altered books are both academic and personal interests that allow her to bridge the gap between her life both inside and out of the Ivory Tower. She is currently at work on a book about religion and twentieth-century literature and a project on the hermeneutics of collage. Jennifer lives in Michigan with her husband, Dale, three-year old son, Nathan, and those pesky cats. **www.questionsconcerningreligion.org**

ABOUT THE AUTHORS

A simple devotion for memory keeping, photography, and the arts ledthis southern California wife and mother, **Sharon Sonneff**, down an unexpected path. After being featured in countless publications, Sharon was inducted into the Creating Keepsakes Hall of Fame. This serendipitous beginning was transformed when her flagship brand, Sonnets, made its debut with a modest introduction of scrapbook papers and stickers. Sonnets is now just a small part of her larger company, Sonnets Studios, which has grown to encompass a substantial body of artwork, several distinct brands, and a vast array of products. Sharon has a passion for watercolors and the lettering arts but also explores various mixed media. When she brings her brush to paper, she also brings her love for nature, architecture, and literature. Her background in interior design and as a colorist also factor into her design savvy. Above all, Sharon's passion is to honor God with her humble gifts and to encourage others to do the same. For more about Sharon Soneff visit her site at **www.sonnetsstudios.com**

Mindy Caliguire is founder and president of Soul Care, **www.soulcare.com**. After the deterioration and eventual recovery of her own soul's health, she became passionate about helping others similarly restore spiritual vitality through connection with God. In addition to her speaking, Soul Care offers beautiful journals, study guides, and other enriching resources. Mindy is a graduate of Cornell University and has held leadership positions at Beacon Community Church near Boston, Massachusetts, and most recently at Willow Creek Community Church in South Barrington, Illinois. She and her husband Jeff have three sons, Jeffrey, Jonathan, and Joshua (the J-Team!).

ACKNOWLEDGMENTS

What an amazing and satisfying experience authoring this book has been, and I'm so entirely grateful to God for inspiring the material in this book and breathing life into it. The way He used this book, intended to spur others on in their spiritual journey, to revitalize my own spiritual life in the process, was a wonderful surprise.

Huge thanks go to each of my contributors, who put their whole heart and spirit into the assignments before them. It is their additions to the book that offer it both artistic range and the unique perspectives of remarkable individuals. That is something that I could never have accomplished on my own. Receiving your projects and then getting to write about them was both an honor and a delight. But most of all, your prayers on my behalf and your commitment to the vision of the book have been priceless.

I'm enormously appreciative to Mindy Caliguire for the insightful and practical help she offered in the form of chapter introductions. How she manages to be so plain-spoken and utterly profound at the same time confounds and stirs me. Every time I had the pleasure of reading the entries she supplied, goose bumps never failed to appear and I was left with a stronger conviction of why faith books and spiritual journals are such a worthy pursuit. The warmth, approachability, and energy she leant this project has meant so much.

More sincere thanks go to my editor at Rockport, Mary Ann Hall. Her editorial experience paired with her kind and calm demeanor took the stress out of what could have been a harried project. The solid direction, availability, and support she provided made this endeavor an enjoyable one, and in the end, a polished one. My appreciation also extends to all those at Rockport whose talented hands touched this project.

Lastly, but never least, my gratitude goes out to my dear husband, Gerry, and my two fabulous kids, Ian and Victoria. This project meant more absence of presence on my part and sacrifices on their part; they never expressed complaint, but to the contrary expressed a belief in this project and a confidence in me to accomplish it. Gerry, your toleration of a laptop in bed with us, and the transformation of our home into a warehouse and shipping outlet of boxes holding artful treasures, shows the kind of patience and forbearance you possess that made me fall in love with you in the first place. All three of you: you are at the core of my every triumph, and my net of comfort in my every shortcoming. Thank you for our lives together of pursuing faith side by side.

—Sharon Soneff

"Oh, magnify the Lord with me, And let us exalt His name together."

PSALM 34:3